PERSONAL
COMMUNICATION
STYLE

PERSONAL COMMUNICATION STYLE

"CONTROL THE IMPRESSION YOU MAKE"

DR. DENNIS BECKER

ISBN: 1500387029
ISBN 13: 9781500387020
Library of Congress Control Number: 2014911967
CreateSpace Independent Publishing Platform
North Charleston, South Carolina

INTRODUCTION

WHAT IS THIS BOOK ABOUT?

This book is about people and the way in which they control the impressions they make on other people; it is about communication style. Now, I realize that could be the beginning of a thick book with single-spaced, small-type printing. The two words *communication* and *style* have given birth to an endless number of manuals. This one is different. In fact, you will be hard pressed to find another like it.

To begin with, it will be helpful to clarify what this book is *not* about. This book is not about leadership style. This book is not about management style. There is a plethora of such books. Most of these seem adequate for identifying leadership and management style. While the words *communication style*, either separately or combined, ignite thoughts of everything from music to dance, to sculpture, to film, and so on, the subject is really none of these. Of course, you can make a great case for any of these modalities of expression. Each is a legitimate form of communication. Each has its own style within the genre. This book is not about any of these or other legitimate forms of communication.

This book is about the communication style that is unique to each human being. This book is about the way you present and project yourself. This book is about the impression that people get from the communication style you use. This book is about the way you speak, the way you listen, the way you look, the way you gesture, the way you move, and more. This could include such things as how your office or work area is designed or decorated, the type of car you drive, the type of house you live in, and so on. This book is about how you can design, develop, and deliver the most comfortable and effective personal communication style for your life. This is a small book about a very big subject.

In many ways, it is the most important subject a person must master. No matter what role you have in life, no matter what age you are, no matter what gender or race or culture you belong to, this book can be helpful to you. However, I am aiming this book particularly at those people who are in leadership or management positions in a work setting somewhere in the United States. That is important to specify. I have been privileged to be helpful to men and women around the world. My firm, the Speech Improvement Company, Inc., has served heads of companies and heads of countries for the past fifty years. Some of my best clients and strongest business relationships are with leaders and managers in the Middle East. Obviously, that is very different from American culture! We all know that there are tremendous cultural differences from what we are used to in places other than the United States. Understanding, respecting, and being able to serve within those differences is vital to any level of success in helping individuals or companies in those various cultures. In this book, however, we will focus on the personal communication styles of individuals who serve as leaders or managers in businesses, industries, corporations, and organizations operating within American culture.

There are also differences within the Unites States, of course. A communication style that resonates in New York may be laughed at or viewed with disdain in Louisiana, for example. Recognizing that and granting the reality of each of those differences, the descriptions and recommendations in this book are based on nearly fifty years of study, research, and practice with leaders and managers throughout the United States. The applications of these descriptions and recommendations will vary, and each person will have to make those determinations.

This book is about how to design, develop, and deliver your personal communication style.

How Is This Book Written?

To some folks this may be a strange, almost silly question. I don't take it lightly at all. It's important to you because your time, interest, effort, and increasingly, your patience and attention may be quite short. This book is written with the KISS model in mind. No, I don't mean, "Keep It Simple, Stupid." I would never call my client or any learner *stupid*. My KISS model is, "Keep It Short and Simple."

I am proud to be the eldest son of nine children born to beautiful, hardworking blue-collar parents. My upbringing was pragmatic and no-nonsense, but filled with humor. Most of this took place in a small town, sixty miles northwest of Philadelphia, called West Reading, Pennsylvania. In 1960 I graduated from West Reading High School and became the first of my family to attend college. I became my family's first academic. Following six years of undergraduate and graduate work at Emerson College in Boston, Massachusetts, I earned a BS in speech and an MA in rhetoric and public address. Emerson is the world's preeminent private school specializing in the communication arts, and alma mater to hundreds of famous theatrical, broadcasting, Internet, print, and electronic communicators. I then studied at Union in Cincinnati, where I earned a PhD in media communications, with a specialty in speaking and listening. I have been president of the Massachusetts Speech Communication Association, president of the New England Speech Association, founder and CEO of the Speech Improvement Company, communication coach to hundreds of leaders and managers, author of a best-selling text book on speech, and author of four other books on communication, as well as instructor at both Harvard and MIT. After nearly fifty years of concentrated professional experience in this field, I feel very comfortable approaching this topic with you.

This book is not an academic treatise. As I mentioned, I am writing this book according to my KISS (Keep It Short and Simple) model. This is especially important for this book. This book is intended to help people in a totally different manner and style than normal academic publications do. This book is not a normal academic publication. It is written in shirtsleeve English using everyday vocabulary and real life examples. If you are a PhD with nearly fifty years of experience in a field, as I am, they say you should know about four hundred thousand words. Indeed, I do know a lot of words. Most of them will not be used in this book. The field of communication studies is divided into researchers and practitioners. I am a practitioner. I respect, read, and use the important work of researchers. However, I am a practitioner who writes and speaks in shirt-sleeve English. I promise you I will not use a two-dollar word when a fifty-cent one will do. You're welcome.

To help us do this, I have asked Monica Murphy (monica@speechimprovement.com) and Laurie Schloff, (laurie@speechimprovement.com) two of the professional communication coaches in my office to provide us with examples of actual clients with whom they have engaged using communication style coaching. Monica is a Senior Coaching Partner/Trainer and has been with The Speech Improvement Company for more than 20 years. She is well known around the world. Her clients frequently call on her for high profile coaching engagements because of her warm and comforting, but direct coaching style. Laurie Schloff is a Senior Coaching Partner with The Speech Improvement Company. She has more than 30 years of experience, Laurie is an experienced professional communication coach and author of three books on communication (*Smart Speaking*, *He And She Talk*, *Speech Gems)* Throughout the book Laurie will offer periodic "gender alerts" related to each style word that is discussed.. .In a later chapter, these coaches will introduce you to a few of their clients who represent a variety of ages, cultures and businesses.. They will describe, in their own words, their personal approach and reaction to communication style coaching. In addition, Laurie will provide "gender alerts" at strategic spots in these pages. Here is her first contribution:

Gender Alerts

Your gender plays a role in determining what is effective. True, gender-based stereotypes, which portray women as the softer sex and males as the stronger sex, have blurred a bit in the past decades. And thankfully, it is now more acceptable for men to shed tears, care about clothing, and nurture babies.

Of course, women have made great strides in the workplace in the past half century. Women now comprise 50 percent of both medical and law school classes. On the not-so-equal side, though, when it comes to running the show, women aren't yet faring as well. Less than 1 percent of CEOs are women. There's an expression from the seventies—"Women belong in the House and the Senate!"

Still, though more women than ever ran for political office in 2010, women hold less than 17 percent of seats in the Senate and House of Representatives.

What is the influence of this imbalance on style and communication style coaching? Though female readers may lean toward choosing a strong, authoritative style, women, unlike men, usually succeed better when they balance a competence-based style with a positive-pathos, approachable style. To a greater degree than men, women are still expected to have it *all*, showing nurturing and pleasing behaviors as well as strong and competent ones.

Our communication research indicates that a woman who is perceived as competent but *not* warm will sooner be called "the word that rhymes with rich" than her "made of steel" male counterpart. As a telling example, during Hillary Clinton's 2008 campaign for presidency, her popularity *increased* when she shed tears at a campaign rally in New Hampshire. In other words, until Ms. Clinton showed her softer side, the American public wasn't comfortable with her ambition. Of course, the style combination of strength and sensitivity works for most males as well and leads to positive collegial and client relationships. My point is simply that in most arenas, men have more style flexibility than women. Women will be judged more positively when they balance traditionally male and female traits.

Why Was This Book Written?

First of all, I wrote it because so many people have asked me for it. My company, the Speech Improvement Company, and our coaches, have been doing communication style coaching for nearly fifteen of the last fifty years we have been in business. We coach leaders of companies, leaders of countries, and others from all walks of life, from every business and industry, and from for-profit and nonprofit organizations all around the world. At this date we are approaching one million people whom we have helped. We are convinced that there are many more people whom we may never meet, yet who could be helped by this book. We want to share communication style coaching with everyone.

Second of all, every person who is in a leadership position, whether public or private, corporate or religious, for-profit or nonprofit, or volunteer or paid, should control his or her communication styles as a basic skill of effective leadership and as a means of making the impression he or she really wants to make.

Third of all, I am a great believer in a quote by St. Francis of Assisi. I first saw it on a desk-sized card nearly forty years ago. It is on the wall in our office to this day. "There is no good in walking somewhere to teach unless we teach as we walk." I, and every member of my company, embrace the truth of these words. I am convinced that it is one of the reasons we have outlasted so many other coaching firms and are now the oldest (and perhaps largest) communication-coaching firm in the world. This book has been written because there are so many folks who will benefit by reading it.

Enjoy and benefit.
Dr. Dennis Becker
dennis@speechimprovement.com

CHAPTER 1

WHAT IS COMMUNICATION STYLE COACHING?

In his book *Style*, Sir Walter Alexander Raleigh (1522 - 1618) described language as having a "chameleon-like" quality. Sir Walter's book is an exhaustive study of the origin, popularity, and decline of the word *style*. Regarding style, he said, "Good style is the greatest of revealers—it lays bare the soul." You must be comfortable with your style. You live and work in the real world. It is not theater. Your listeners, unlike the audience in a theater, do not suspend reality. They take what you give them as *you*. What and how you communicate is what others use to assess and describe you. What and how you communicate reveals much of who you are in real life. The ability to be natural, to be who you are, and not to be phony, is most people's goal, especially those in leadership and management positions. Those positions carry enough responsibility in their own ways. It is far too challenging to also be worried about being something that you have to fake or that is not comfortable for you. Not only can it be uncomfortable, but it can also be downright discomforting to try and match a particular leadership or management style that has been dictated or described in a textbook. There is truth in a favorite quote of mine: "Life is not a dress rehearsal." We do not get a second chance to go around in life. It is incumbent upon each of us to do the best we can every day, to project our best, most sincere, and most authentic selves. That is what communication style coaching is all about. It is most successful when you are truly comfortable with the communication techniques you use to create the impression you want others to have of you. This is even truer in today's world than it was in the time of Sir Walter Alexander Raleigh.

Perhaps all this consideration of style began with Aristotle (384 BC–322 BC), the student of Plato, who is generally accepted as the formulator of persuasion and the art of speaking. His world-shaping book, *Ars Rhetorica*, or *The Art of Rhetoric*, was not written as a book at all. It was a treatise, a collection of notes to his students regarding his teachings. It has been divided into three books. In book three he discusses style. He deals mostly with figures of speech, such as metaphors and similes, clarity in organization, and pronunciation of words. Each of these was rooted in contemporary Greek society. However, the treatise still holds a major place in the human society of our time. Much of what you will learn from this book has its roots in the teachings of Aristotle.

In keeping with the KISS model, let's define style coaching as a "process for designing, developing, and delivering oneself in a comfortable, controlled manner." For those of you who would like a broader framework, I offer the following: Wikipedia, the popular online encyclopedia, lists at least 133 topics under the category of human communication. These subcategories range from voice to neurolinguistic programming, from nonverbal communication to social skills, from social conceptions of the face to answering yes-or-no questions, and many more. Almost any of them could be a subcategory of style coaching. Of course, we don't focus on that many. The actual number, however, depends on such variables as the needs of the client, time considerations, levels of commitment, learning capabilities, and even geography. It can be difficult to conduct style coaching when the client and coach are in different countries. It is certainly not impossible. We do it all the time. Suffice to say that there are many variables that we must consider.

In this book, we will look very closely at sixteen of the most prominent and recognizable variables in the perception of personal communication style. They are the following: articulation, pronunciation, rate, pace, voice, speech, ethos, pathos, logos, vocal variety, gestures, facial expression, body language, listening, paralanguage and color words.

These are terms that will be repeated throughout this book and used to explain suggested techniques. Where there is need to modify the following definitions in particular circumstances, it will be noted. I urge you to become familiar with these as you go through the book. The differences between them can be subtle, yet important.

Vocal variety is the absence of sameness in the voice during speech. The word *vocal* means of the voice. This differs from speech. Voice is the sound you are able to produce. Speech is what you do with the voice you have produced. Vocal variety refers to such things as volume, quality, and pitch. A monotonous speaker really isn't monotonous, literally speaking. The roots *mono* and *tonus* imply that the voice has produced only one tone over a period of time. Actually, when a speaker is called monotonous, he or she is actually repeating a series of vocal and speech techniques over and over without variation. Vocal variety will help alleviate monotony and boredom.

Color words are any words that a speaker says differently than other words in the same sentences. Any word can be a color word. The term originated during the era when television programs were broadcast in black and white. When color programming was introduced, it brought a whole new excitement and a new emphasis to the programs. Hence, color words bring an emphasis, an excitement, or a specialness to the word or phrase that the speaker uses to make a point. The content is no longer simply black and white; it is colorful. Color words are selectively emphasized by speakers in order to identify the most important words in the sentence. A color word is the word that modifies or activates the key thought. Color words can be nouns, verbs, pronouns, adjectives, adverbs, articles, or prepositions. Color words can be produced in several ways. A speaker can use volume, inflection, speech, or duration. Duration as a speech technique may be unfamiliar to many of you. Duration is the length of time the speaker takes to pronounce a word or sound. Typically, duration involves prolonging a sound in a word. Robin Williams used duration in the 1987 movie *Good Morning, Vietnam*, when he began his radio broadcast by saying, "Gooooood morning, Vietnam!" He brought duration to the first vowel sound in the word *good*. Perhaps a more contemporary example of duration can be found in Michael Buffer, the ring announcer. As a boxing match is about to begin, he proclaims, "Let's get ready to rumblllllle!" He brings duration to the last sound in the word *rumble*. And many of us are familiar with Steve Martin's famous line, "Excuuuuuuse me!" Here, again, duration is used to color the word *excuse*.

Articulation is the ability of a speaker to accurately produce a single sound, such as the sound of the letter *r* or the sound of a *th* or any of the other forty to fifty sounds in the American dialect of English. Proper articulation involves one or more of the six articulators in the mouth: lips, teeth, tongue, velum (soft pallet), pharyngeal wall (back of the throat), and lower jaw.

Pronunciation is the ability to bring the articulated sounds together to produce a word that others can understand.

Rate is the speed at which a speaker puts words together. The normal rate of speed of speaking in a business presentation is approximately 150 to 160 words per minute. This can vary, of course. Rate is measured in words per minute.

Pace is the speed at which a speaker puts thoughts together. It is controlled by the amount of time a speaker pauses between thoughts. This can vary greatly and is not measured in the same way that rate is measured. The speaker's purpose and intent, the listener's level of knowledge of the subject, the setting, and many other variables will dictate the appropriate length of a pause. The pause in speaking that a speaker creates between thoughts dictates the pace.

Body language is the intentional or unintentional movement of parts of the body that convey meaning to others. We will extract from this general definition both facial expressions and gestures of hands and arms. These will be given special attention.

Facial expressions are the movement of parts of the face that convey meaning to others. The face contains a potential for sending information that is unlike any other part of the body. The eyes and the mouth are the most dominant and expressive.

Gestures are the movements of hands and arms that convey meaning to others. Typically, these two components of gesture are the most commonly used by speakers and therefore will be given special attention.

Voice is the sound you are able to produce. We will consider the quality of voice, volume, breathing for vocal production, and modulation.

Speech is what you do with your voice. We will consider articulation, pronunciation, inflection, and speed as elements to be used in creating the desired communication style.

Ethos is the cumulative quality of character, credibility, and reputation possessed by each person. When a speaker has *ethos*, the mere mention of his or her name is sufficient to inspire action.

Pathos is the cumulative quality of emotion as manifest in the speaker's actual demeanor and presentation. The ability to move others to action through the use of emotions is pathos.

Logos is the use of logic to move others to action.

Paralanguage is the production of sounds not necessarily identifiable as words, such as grunts, laughter, or the production of actual words or phrases such as "Oh I see," "Tell me more," "Who said that?" and so on. These phrases should never exceed three words. That is, effective paralanguage is perceived as an expression of interest, not an interruption.

Listening: The is the ability to not only to "hear", which is a physical attribute, but to also to be able to dedicate attentive and evaluative capabilities to an interaction.

CHAPTER 2

HOW DOES IT WORK?

Conceptually, style coaching is easy to describe. Remember, the definition is, "the process of designing, developing, and delivering oneself in a comfortable and controlled manner." Let's look at the key words:

Process: No one comes to style coaching without already having a style of personal or professional communication. Whether you are aware of your style or not, you have one. Your friends, neighbors, and colleagues all know what it is. Some of them will recognize it and not want to be your friend, neighbor, or colleague. Some will recognize it and want to be your friend, neighbor, and colleague because of it. Most people will not consciously recognize your communication style, per se; to them it will just be the way you are. They will like or dislike you on those terms, with no overt reference to your communication style. The point here is that everyone has a communication style. A process of development has already taken place in order for you to have your communication style. A plethora of books, research studies, and multitudes of experts have investigated and explored the process that humans go through to develop their communication styles. The truth is that most people do little or nothing to actively or consciously shape the process of this development. The closest attempt to consciously control and shape personal communication style seems to take place, or at least begin, in junior high school. This is the period when adolescents are going through the process of self-identification and labeling. They become extremely sensitive to dress, hair, makeup, vocabulary, body language, and more in the effort to either fit in or stand out. This is, in fact, an experience in style coaching. This process can be as short as a few months or as long as a few years. And it is a process. I'm sure most of us can remember some awful or wonderful thing we learned to say, a way to walk, a way to wear clothes, certain hair styles, and so on that made us feel good.

In our work with adults, it is also a process. During communication style coaching with adults, this process typically evolves in as short a time as two months or as long a period as six to eight months. As with adolescents, there are many variables, but this is the normal time frame in which the person being coached feels differences and those differences are observed by others. It is not a technique. It is not a philosophy. It is not an attitude. It is not verbal or nonverbal. Communication style coaching is a process that includes all of these and more.

Design: Once it has been determined that style coaching is appropriate for someone (this process will be discussed in detail elsewhere), we ask the client to answer one question. The answer provides the frame in which style coaching takes place. That question is, "What two words would you like other people to use when describing your communication style after they have heard you in a meeting or delivering a presentation? They are meeting with others, you are not present, and your name comes up. What two words would you like them to use when describing you?"

The tendency is for the client to respond immediately with two words. How difficult can it be to come up with only two words? That is often the thinking when style coaching is first introduced. However, because style coaching is intended to apply in both business and personal settings, and because these two words are not intended to change (unless traumatic events occur), it is imperative that the client takes the time to think about which words to choose. Those who make an immediate choice do so usually because it's easy and quick. However, this is not a good idea. The client is urged to consult with business colleagues, family, and friends. Explain and share the plans for style coaching. Ask others to give their suggestions for style words. Some clients may find it uncomfortable to ask others. If so, accept it. It is most important that the client him or herself be comfortable and in agreement with the words chosen.

The first word should be one that the client has heard before in reference to him or herself, maybe many times. It feels good to hear others refer to you this way. It may appear in performance reviews or in other work-related settings. This first word may also be heard in informal settings like family gatherings or dinner parties. This first word should be one that the client is happy to hear and is comfortable being referred to in that way. This word is strength. Keep it. It may be that neither the coach nor the client understands the nuances of how the client creates this impression. That is not important at this point. If it works and the client likes it, keep it.

The second word should be one that the client has not heard in reference to him or herself but would like to hear. It may be a quality or a technique seen in a colleague. The desire is not to be that person, but rather to possess the particular communication skill of that person. This clearly becomes the area of greatest growth opportunity. The second word is often a balance to the first word. That is, if the first word chosen is *dynamic*, the second word may well be something like *approachable*. If the first word is *dynamic"* and the second word is *"enthusiastic*, the resulting style may be too overpowering. Some clients find it helpful to refer to one word as a business word and the other word as a personal word. It is strictly a matter of choice determined by the circumstances of the client's environment and the desired effect.

When the two words have been chosen, they are shared with the coach. The coach must then help define the words to the client's satisfaction. This is an important part of the process. Both the coach and the client must have clear agreement on the definition, implications, and possible inferences of each word.

The coaching and learning process may challenge and call into question long-standing communication beliefs and behaviors. In some cases this can raise issues of personal values and attitudes, some of which may need to change. Changes of this sort can be difficult and unsettling. An individual has a personality that includes elements such as verbal and nonverbal behaviors by which others identify that person. These observations are then totaled up into descriptions such as, "he's very laid-back," or "she's a very sensitive person," or "he's quite aggressive," or "she has an outgoing personality." We all use this kind of language when describing other people. We are describing their personalities as we experience them in normal circumstances. What happens when the circumstances are not normal? What happens when things become stressful? Each of us has a secondary personality. This personality is made up of another set of behaviors. In some cases these other behaviors are quite different. Sometimes they are only slightly different. Other people see these differences and can tell that you are stressed or somehow "not your usual self." They are witnessing your secondary personality. For some people, there may also be a third personality, which is activated by extreme stress or incredible joy. How are these layers of personality formed? How do we each decide to switch from layer to layer? What influences the behaviors that present themselves as part of each layer? These are questions that psychiatrists and psychologists wrestle with every day. Why does all this concern us? How does it affect style coaching? Specifically, how does this affect the design of style words? There is an important connection. First of all, behaviors on each of these levels will communicate something to those around us. Second of all, the style words that are chosen must not contradict the basic values we carry through life. Beneath the layers of personality we all have lies the persona. The persona is the vault in which we each keep our core set of values. These are beliefs we live by. Some of them have been forming since childhood. Some of them have been shaped by life events. Some are the result of relationships and experiences we have had. In some people, these are so deeply ingrained that we are not even aware of their presence. "It's just the way I am," as people frequently say. These core beliefs and values that are housed in the persona are the roots of the behaviors that blossom in the layers and branches of our personalities. The two style words that form the framework for style coaching must be compatible with those core values and beliefs. Any significant incongruence will make it very difficult for both the coach and the client to design, develop, and especially deliver the communication techniques that support each style word.

In the process of designing a fertile comfort zone for the client, it sometimes becomes evident that in order for the communication techniques to become natural, there must be a change in the beliefs and values rooted in the persona. Style coaching doesn't demand life-altering changes. It does require that the client recognize those core beliefs and values and take them into consideration when selecting two style words. If the words are not reconciled to the beliefs, the communication techniques that are being introduced to deliver the desired impression will feel uncomfortable and unnatural.

We have found, however, that clients tend to choose words that are a slight stretch from their normal communication styles. When the words represent a major change, the coach and the client must recognize this. They must discuss the implications the change carries. It's important that the client doesn't get set up for disappointment or failure. Occasionally, a client who is shy and retiring will say, "I'd like to be just like Jay Leno or Joan Rivers." While it may be possible, simply adopting two style words may not be nearly enough. It becomes the responsibility of the coach to assess what is reasonably possible within the frame of variables the client and coach face. Challenges such as available time, temperament, cost, practice, and learning style will all have an impact on success.

So, the choice of style words as part of the style coaching is a very important first step. It is best for the client to take time, ask friends and colleagues, and envision the settings and persons that are most important and where communication will be critical before answering the question, "What two words would you like others to use when describing your communication style?"

When these two words have been selected, they form a frame in which all coaching takes place. Every communication technique that is identified must be selected because it supports one of the two style words. Of course, every communication technique selected must also be palatable to the client. He or she must be comfortable using them. These techniques will be exhibited in the various layers of their personalities. This is the reason for our brief exploration of personality and persona.

Development: During this phase of the process, learning is focused on acquiring the specific communication techniques that will help create the desired impression (the two style words). A valuable part of developing the appropriate approaches and techniques for success is to conduct an oral 360 review. The key word here is oral. The traditional, multipage, carefully worded, and written 360 review is only marginally helpful for style coaching. In an oral 360 review, the client is asked to provide the contact information for three or four people who are familiar with and important to him or her. Typically, it is helpful to identify a person who reports to the client, another who is a peer of the client, and someone to whom the client reports. It is also helpful to be able to speak with individuals from outside the work sphere. Because style coaching is normally done as part of business or professional development, these nonbusiness contacts can be excluded. However, whenever possible, names of non-work-related individuals should be added to the three directly related contacts. Communication techniques that are developed as part of style coaching are intended to be utilized everywhere. They should be effective in both business and nonbusiness settings. If this is not done, it is inevitable that others will get the impression that they are dealing with two different people. If you communicate differently in the business setting than you do in the nonbusiness setting, there will be suspicion as to which is the real you. Having said that, of course, there is some flexibility here. No one uses the exact language in their parents' home that they use with their close friends in a bar. We all try to dress a bit differently when we are at a town hall meeting than when we are alone at a beach house. The point here is that the two style words, while they may be quite different, should not compel you to feel like you are leading two lives, that you have to have two sets of clothing, two vastly different vocabularies, etc. You should feel both comfortable with and capable of living within the identified range of the two style words.

The reason for conducting the 360 review orally is to allow for a free flow of thoughts from the interviewee regarding their observations and recommendations. A more-traditional, written 360 review does not allow for this face-to-face or voice-to-voice interaction. Hence, the coach must draw conclusions in a somewhat restricted fashion. To facilitate this, the client is asked to inform the three or four individuals that the coach will be contacting them. The client is directed to ask the interviewee to reserve ten to fifteen minutes for the oral 360 conversation. This time frame is important. It assures the interviewee that it is not a huge time commitment. It further allows for a focused conversation. During the 360 interviews, the coach asks two simple questions:

1. From your knowledge of _____, what communication skill is he or she particularly good at?
2. From your knowledge of _____, what communication skill would he or she be benefitted most by strengthening?

When these answers are provided, the coach often finds it helpful to ask for an example of the behavior identified. This leads to better information and insights that can be factored into style coaching. The coach may find it helpful to clarify whether the interviewee observes or interacts with the client in a group or one on one setting, or a formal or informal setting. These various bits of data are very valuable as part of the coaching and should be gathered at the beginning of the coaching process. The oral 360 should be conducted prior to beginning the structured phase of coaching. I cannot overstate the importance of this being an oral exchange between the coach and the interviewee. The communication coach should be listening for key words and phrases, cautious use of words, and attempts to mask undesirable characteristics or to highlight unrepresentative behavior.

This development phase contains the activities practice, feedback, and coaching. The coach must consider all the variables of teaching and learning in order to select appropriate techniques. It's a bit like the computer experience we all know. You click on a word such as *services* and a menu of *services* drops down, inviting you to choose the appropriate one to meet your needs. The coach can likewise choose from a menu of communication techniques related to a style word. The coach, having considered the variables, chooses the two or three techniques that will help the client exhibit that style. If a particular technique is not comfortable or doesn't work, the coach can return to the menu again, and select new communication techniques. This process continues until the client is comfortable implementing the techniques supporting the specific style word. The number of techniques needed to develop a style word is completely flexible. Typically, we find that three to five new verbal techniques suffice. Developing a comfortable mastery of the chosen communication techniques is the main goal of this phase. Coaching plays a critical role in the process. Coaching is not training, teaching, telling, inspiring, motivating, or persuading. Each of these is an individual modality and could stand alone as a skill set. For our purposes, it is accepted that coaching involves all of these. The unique distinction for us is that coaching is a one-on-one experience. Three other modalities of communication are:

Telling, which is simply passing information from one source to another with no requirements for sender or receiver save clarity. For example, telling looks something like this: "Today we will review the 6 articulators required for speaking clearly."

Teaching, which is the passing of information or ideas from one source to another for purposes of learning and education. An example of teaching might be the following: "To articulate speech clearly it is important to utilize the six articulators. These are the lips, teeth, tongue, lower jaw, velum, and pharyngeal wall. What are the six articulators and why are they important?" Then the learner, the object of teaching, replies with opportunity for questions and interaction for understanding.

Training is combination of telling and teaching with the addition of demonstrating what has been learned. For example, a command in training might be: "Now that you know what the articulators are, please demonstrate how each contributes to articulation."

Coaching demands a more intimate relationship with the client. Coaching demands that you customize both the content to be learned and the process by which it will be delivered. Coaches must get to know and understand the client in a manner and to a depth that is not necessary or possible in a group training session.

Two broad coaching approaches are *outside in* and *inside out*. Both of these are viable and valuable. Style coaching utilizes only the *inside out* approach. Here's the difference:

Outside in gives the client the communication techniques that are obvious, visible to others. The client learns, and uses, only those aspects of the technique that are evident to another person. It is not necessary or desirable for the client to analyze or internalize the elements of the technique. *Outside in* is the approach that is most commonly employed, for example, when the client is facing a one time speaking experience such as a conference or convention presentation, and requests help getting through only this event. For instance, in an industry conference of a thousand people, an *outside in approach to* coaching could include points like the following:

1. Don't stand behind the lectern
2. When moving across the platform, stop and face the listeners whenever making a theme statement.
3. Move eye contact across the auditorium in a z-shaped movement.

This style of coaching is didactic and directive more than Socratic and reflective. It is intended to give the client the outward techniques with no attempt to solicit interaction or dialogue. *Outside in* coaching is most effective in situations where time is short or the client has a limited need.

Inside out is the opposite. This approach is appropriate when the client needs to analyze and understand the intricacies of certain communication techniques. The client should have a thorough understanding of why a technique has been chosen, as well as how it is used. The term *inside out* is indicative of the need to internalize the technique. For instance: in an industry conference of a thousand people, coaching could include these tips:

1. To appear *approachable* (one of the selected style words), it will be important not to stand behind the lectern. It will become a wall between you and your listener. It may also convey a lack of confidence or insecurity.
2. Move across the platform at a slower than faster pace. You can look pensive or reflective as you move. When you are about to make a statement that you believe is really important for your audience to understand, stop walking, gently turn to face them, and make the statement. It will show personal commitment and a desire to be open with them.
3. It is not necessary to maintain eye contact at all times. As you move gently across the platform, it is acceptable to look at the floor, ceiling, and so on, as though you are thinking and being open to ideas. Stop moving every six to eight steps. Face the listeners while expressing a complete thought before moving on. It shows an understanding and comfort with the topic.

Of course, this is not a script. It is an indication that much more explanation and rationale is required for the client to understand and commit to the communication technique being introduced and how it exemplifies the style word in question: *approachable*.

The key point here is that *outside in* is direct, didactic, and one-sided. *Inside out* is less direct, inductive, and solicits frequent input from the client. Demonstration of the communication techniques being taught may be part of both coaching styles. Communication style coaching honors both of these styles, but definitely favors *inside out*. Actually, the coach may find it helpful to use both styles, as the client's personality and learning style require during this development phase of learning.

Delivery: The ultimate responsibility for delivering the communication techniques is with the client. He or she must be able to exhibit the correct techniques in a comfortable manner. The delivery must fit the situation. The delivery must be consistent. In short, the delivery of the techniques learned must do many things in order to convey the desired impression of style. This is why it is so important that the techniques chosen must be both appropriate for the style words that have been chosen, comfortable for the client to deliver, and there must be clear, agreed understanding between coach and client.

As an individual's style coaching is designed and delivered, it is important that both client and coach remain cognizant of the need to deliver the chosen style in every setting, both personal and professional, and, again, the importance of selecting appropriate style words. Style coaching does not imply that the two words reflect different styles of communication for business and nonbusiness settings. In fact, one of the main goals of style coaching is to find style words that allow for the client to be comfortable communicating either in business or nonbusiness settings. Realistically, of course, we all know that the differences in these two settings can be dramatic. This may be a good thing. No one wants to be chastised in a personal setting with, "don't talk to me like I work for you," or, in a work setting with, "I'm your colleague, not your cousin, I'd appreciate a bit more respect." Ouch! The style words chosen should allow for appropriate applications in each setting. This may require slight modifications in language, inflection, facial expression, and so on. What should be avoided is anything that causes the client to have the feeling or give the impression of acting or being two different people.

I am reminded of the many times when coaching someone for a presentation of some sort, and the client wants to know how to be in that particular setting. "Be yourself" is not a frivolous reply. It's also not easy to do. Most presenters believe that it is necessary to have a special demeanor or style for a special presentation. Clients often feel that their upcoming presentations are a special event. They buy new clothes, get a special haircut, etc. While there may well be aspects of the upcoming events that are special, it is equally important that the speaker be as comfortable and natural as possible. New shoes and new clothing can prove to be uncomfortable and not natural feeling. Yes, there may be something special about the presentation. Speakers are not always in control of certain aspects and expectations for delivery of their presentations. However, speakers are always in control of intrapersonal aspects and their own expectations of their deliveries. Goals for delivery should be relaxation, poise, purpose, comfort, confidence, and effectiveness. The truth is that every time you talk, you are making a presentation. You are taking the thoughts from your head and presenting them to someone else. I should repeat that: *Every time you talk, you are making a presentation.* If you are comfortable and effective in one setting, then communication style coaching can help you be comfortable and effective in any setting. I realize this sounds simple. It can be quite difficult. Both client and coach must agree that style coaching is most effective when the delivery of the learned communication techniques can be carried through both business and personal settings. Of course, there are differences. Those differences must be identified and considered when choosing style words. The goal here is *designing* and *developing* a style that is real, visceral, and practical for the client to *deliver*. The techniques learned must blend seamlessly from business to nonbusiness settings. If this does not happen, the client will feel as though he or she is faking, acting, not being natural. While differences in the business and nonbusiness settings may be broad, the differences in the techniques learned should be subtle. Chosen styles should be delivered seamlessly in any setting, from personal to professional.

Delivery is the practice phase when the client is refining the delivery of the communication techniques learned. Learning the techniques and liking the techniques contribute to the intellectual, emotional, and physical ability to deliver the techniques. Despite these good feelings, it is not uncommon to hear a client say something like, "it just doesn't feel natural." What does this mean? What is a natural behavior? It sounds like a simple question. A simple definition could be, natural is what you are accustomed to. You walk the way you do because it is natural to you. You talk the way you talk because it's natural to you. The truth is you walk the way you do because you learned it. It is a habit. The truth is that you speak the way you do because it is how you learned it. You imitated, you were taught, and as a result your speech became a habitual behavior to you. You brush your teeth, comb your hair, use your fork, and perform many more behaviors routinely because it is the way you learned to do it. They are natural to you. The truth is that they have become habitual. They feel natural to you. If you break your arm and have to learn to do some of these things with your other arm, suddenly these routine behaviors feel very awkward, uncomfortable, and even ineffective. They are no longer natural because they are no longer habitual. So, what is natural is what is habitual to you. The same is true about the delivery of the newly learned communication techniques you will use to shape and express your chosen communication style. It takes some time for them to become habitual behaviors to become natural.

Clients often struggle to find patience that is needed for these new communication techniques to become comfortable, habitual, and natural. That's natural! When we are children, especially young children, it is much easier for us to develop habitual behaviors quickly. A child is like the white board found in so many offices. An infant's white board is blank. It is open and inviting the world to write on it. Parents, teachers, family members, other children, and even television programming, write on the child's white board. Along the way, some of the markings on the white board get erased or written over. Some stay, and stay, and stay into adulthood.

So, when a coach meets a client, the coach is meeting someone whose white board has a great deal of markings on it. Some of them have been there for a long time and have become comfortable and habitual. They seem natural. There may be little or no room on the white board to write new things. Perhaps it will be necessary to erase some of the old habits in order to develop some desired new habits. Just as with an office white board, it's not always easy to erase old things. They may be stained on the board. They can be erased but it takes a bit of time and special attention. Then new things can be put on the white board. Learning new communication techniques is the same. Actually, a person's communication style is normally made up of things that have been on their white board for a long time, reinforced by practice and use. They may be very difficult to erase or modify. So patience is required on the part of both the client and the coach. My grandmother always told me, "Patience is a virtue; possess it if you can. Seldom found in woman, but never found in man."

CHAPTER 3
WHAT ARE STYLE WORDS?

The last thirty years have seen design-your-own jeans, diets, vacations, even eye color, and so much more. Currently, we are on the outer limits of being able to design children. As amazing and as controversial as it is, it may soon be possible to predetermine the gender, and more, of your children before birth. Humans have been designing animals for generations by breeding the dogs, cats, and other animals we domesticate. Can human cloning be far behind? Humans can be a very self-centered species. Perhaps all this is merely a contemporary technological expression of Darwin's theory. So, why not choose your own communication style? It is possible, and it starts with choosing style words.

Style words extend your ability to design your own communication style. Style words, in themselves, are not new. Each of us has lain in bed, or looked in the mirror, thinking about both how we look or would like to look, and ascribing words to it. It was about junior high school when focus on appearance peaked and blossomed into a similar concern about the impression we make. Eventually, the way we looked was coupled with the way we spoke. The words and phrases we used and the sound of our voices became points of focus and concern. The idea of fitting in collided with the idea of standing out. As the Yul Brynner sang in the *King and I*, "'Tis a puzzlement."

Style words provide a person with opportunity and ability to design their own impression. Style words must be thoughtfully and strategically selected. Communication style coaching is the path to creating the way you want others to think of you. Coaching a person along the path of communication style is a responsibility that should only be undertaken after critical discussion with the client to ensure that the two chosen style words are truly within the grasp of the client. Coaching a person along this path also requires that the coach understand the meaning of the style words in their own mind as well as in the mind of the client. In addition, of course, a qualified coach will know the appropriate communication techniques that will breathe life into the style words.

When choosing style words, there is a process of investigation, exploration, and assessment that the client goes through. Some words that flow from this process are not style words. One of the most frequently cited words of this type is *knowledgeable*. It sounds reasonable. After all, being known as a knowledgeable person actually seems desirable. However, as a style word for a person who is just entering the work force or who has entered a new position from a different discipline, a *knowledgeable* communication style could come across as a bit defensive. It could promote a mind-set that you have to prove that you are knowledgeable or you wouldn't have been promoted into the position. Though on the other hand, a case could possibly be made for *knowledgeable* as a style word. There are many factors to weigh. Both client and coach must assess each word proposed for applicability to the real world of the client.

Of all the words we have heard suggested as style words, from the many clients who have gone through style coaching over the past fifteen years, there are seven that emerge as most frequently as selected by leaders of companies and leaders of countries.

These are: *approachable, authoritative, comfortable, confident, enthusiastic, motivational,* and *personable.*

Over the past fifteen years or so, hundreds of individuals have been part of the communication style coaching learning experience. They represent a wide variety of businesses, industries, government, private sector, for profit and nonprofit organizations. Both genders are represented. Approximately 65 percent have been male and approximately 35 percent have been female. Their titles vary in each company. Typical position titles are CEO, COO, CFO, CIO, CTO, president, senior vice-president, VP, director, and senior manager. In the world of politics these titles do not apply, obviously. However, politics is as much of an image game as it is a talent game. Political positions almost always require the building and careful management of image and impression. Political titles can vary greatly. In the United States we have coached neighborhood chairmen, local representatives, state representatives and senators, governors and national office holders as well. In all these settings, with all these titles, in a wide range of different disciplines, those who chose style words tended to choose the above-mentioned words most frequently. It is worth repeating that even when the style words were the same, the coaching, learning, and application of the communication techniques were different. Here are the explanations of the seven most frequently desired communication styles of leaders from all walks of life:

Authoritative: This communication style is not the same as *authoritarian*—the heavy-handed style that says, "my way or the highway." An *authoritative* person is someone who other people feel they can come to with a concern or problem and the *authoritative* person will either solve or provide guidance to solving the problem. In any case, the time spent interacting with an *authoritative* person always feels beneficial and productive.

Approachable: An *approachable* person gives the impression of someone who would be kind, respectful and receptive if another person approached him or her. He or she does not appear standoffish or aloof, but friendly, open, and safe.

Comfortable: This person seems easy to be around and at ease with him or herself. Movements, vocabulary, and topics discussed all indicate a person who is self-aware and comfortable interacting with others.

Confident: This word can be understood to mean showing confidence or instilling confidence. Both are viable. Here we will emphasize the intent of showing confidence. We recognize the value in being able to instill confidence in others. We also acknowledge the importance of creating the feeling of confidence within oneself. These qualities and competencies are indeed admirable. They would normally contribute to creating a confident impression in the marketplace. Here we will focus on those communication techniques that project an air of self-confidence to others.

Enthusiastic: This style exudes energy. There seems to be an ever-present sense of excitement and joy. An enthusiastic person is almost always positive about issues, and can hardly wait to get started with undertakings.

Motivational: This style is usually easily recognizable. This person is able to create an environment of wanting to do something. This style creates an impression of emotional commitment. Most importantly, this style also communicates what to do with that energy.

Personable: This person is the type you have to get to know. While he or she may seem uncomfortable or aloof at the initial meeting, once you get to know him or her, the person may be quite nice and easy to be with.

These are the most frequently chosen style words that have been selected by executive clients over the past fifteen years. There are others, of course. Each must be selected to fit the needs of the individual client. Because communication style coaching is totally unique to each person, it is possible that different people may have the same two style words but create that style with different sets of techniques. In the next chapter we will review each of these style words and describe the various communication techniques that are most frequently used to create the desired impression.

It is important to reiterate that the communication techniques found in these pages are those most frequently ascribed to the particular style words with which they appear. The same style words selected by a different person may require a different set of techniques. Each person is unique. The strength and uniqueness of communication style coaching is that it custom fits each person.

In order for communication style coaching to be successful for you, it is very important that you choose style words that you believe in, are comfortable for you, and most of all, that you can deliver without feeling like you're acting. Remember, style coaching is designed to allow you to be effective and real. It is not about acting, nor is it feeling that you are trying to be something or someone you are not. Your friends and business associates know you in the reality of everyday life. They do not suspend disbelief, as in the theater or in the movies. In order to be productive for you, your style words must be comfortable for you.

CHAPTER 4

HOW ARE STYLE WORDS MODIFIED?

Everything communicates something. When the client selects style words, it must be recognized that the environment within which he or she will be communicating is going to dictate some of the elements of his or her style, which must be carefully evaluated. These may include such things as hairstyle, clothing, personal hygiene, and other characteristics of the surroundings. Experience has shown that there are many experts who are able to advise on these items. Here we are focused on the very personal characteristics of how a person speaks and behaves in order to create the particular impression indicated by the chosen style words.

Each of the seven style words we introduced in the last chapter will be filtered through and modified by sixteen of the most important variables in the communication of personal communication style. These are:

Articulation, pronunciation, rate, pace, voice, speech, ethos, pathos, logos, vocal variety, gestures, facial expression, body language, color words, paralanguage, and listening.

Some of these variables will be familiar to you. Those which are not will be carefully defined. Each of them is a minute aspect of communication. I am describing them individually to provide perspective on how each effects the intended style. These are terms that will be repeated and applied to each technique and style word. Where there is need to depart from the following definitions, that will be noted. I urge you to become familiar with these. The differences between and among them are subtle yet important.

Vocal variety is the absence of sameness in the voice during speech. The word *vocal* means of the voice. This differs from speech. Voice is the sound you are able to produce. Speech is what you do with the voice you have produced. Vocal variety refers to such things as volume, quality, and pitch. A monotonous speaker really isn't monotonous, literally speaking. The roots *mono* and *tonus* imply that the voice has produced only one tone over a period of time. Actually, when a speaker is called monotonous, he or she is actually repeating a series of vocal and speech techniques over and over without variation. Vocal variety will help alleviate monotony and boredom.

Color words are any words that a speaker says differently than other words in the same sentences. Any word can be a color word. The term originated during the era when television programs were broadcast in black and white. When color programming was introduced, it brought a whole new excitement and a new emphasis to the programs. Hence, color words bring an emphasis, an excitement, a specialness to the word or phrase that the speaker uses to make a point. The content is no longer simply black and white; it is colorful. Color words are selectively emphasized by speakers in order to identify the most important words in the sentence. A color word is the word that modifies or activates the key thought. Color words can be nouns, verbs, pronouns, adjectives, adverbs, articles, or prepositions. Color words can be produced in several ways. A speaker can use volume, inflection, speech, or duration. Duration as a speech technique may be unfamiliar to many of you. Duration is the length of time the speaker takes to pronounce a word or sound. Typically, duration involves prolonging a sound in a word. Robin Williams used duration in the 1987 movie *Good Morning, Vietnam* when he began his radio broadcast by saying, "Gooooood morning, Vietnam!" He brought duration to the first vowel sound in the word *good*. Perhaps a more contemporary example of duration can be found in Michael Buffer, the ring announcer. As a boxing match is about to begin, he proclaims, "Let's get ready to rumblllllle!" He brings duration to the last sound in the word *rumble*. And many of us are familiar with Steve Martin's famous line, "Excuuuuuuse me!" Here, again, duration is used to color the word *excuse*.

Articulation is the ability of a speaker to accurately produce a single sound, such as the sound of the letter *r* or the sound of a *th* or any of the other forty to fifty sounds in the American dialect of English. Proper articulation involves one or more of the six articulators in the mouth: lips, teeth, tongue, velum (soft pallet), pharyngeal wall (back of the throat), and lower jaw.

Pronunciation is the ability to bring the articulated sounds together to produce a word that others can understand.

Rate is the speed at which a speaker puts words together. The normal rate of speed of speaking in a business presentation is approximately 150 to 200 words per minute. This can vary, of course. Rate is measured in words per minute.

Pace is the speed at which a speaker puts thoughts together. It is controlled by the amount of time a speaker pauses between thoughts. This can vary greatly and is not measured in the same way that rate is measured. The speaker's purpose and intent, the listener's level of knowledge of the subject, the setting, and many other variables will dictate the appropriate length of a pause. The pause in speaking that a speaker creates between thoughts dictates the pace.

Body language is the intentional or unintentional movement of parts of the body that convey meaning to others. We will extract from this general definition both facial expressions and gestures of hands and arms. These will be given special attention.

Facial expressions are the movement of parts of the face that convey meaning to others. The face contains a potential for sending information that is unlike any other part of the body. The eyes and the mouth are the most dominant and expressive.

Gestures are the movements of hands and arms that convey meaning to others. Typically, these two components of gesture are the most commonly used by speakers and therefore will be given special attention.

Voice is the sound you are able to produce. We will consider the quality of voice, volume, breathing for vocal production, and modulation.

Speech is what you do with your voice. We will consider articulation, pronunciation, inflection, and speed as elements to be used in creating the desired communication style.

Ethos is the cumulative quality of character, credibility, and reputation possessed by each person. When a speaker has *ethos*, the mere mention of his or her name is sufficient to inspire action.

Pathos is the cumulative quality of emotion as manifest in the speaker's actual demeanor and presentation. The ability to move others to action through the use of emotions is pathos.

Logos is the use of logic to move others to action, understanding, or acceptance.

Paralanguage is the production of sounds not necessarily identifiable as words, such as grunts, laughter, or the production of actual words or phrases such as "Oh I see," "Tell me more," "Who said that?" and so on. These phrases should never exceed three words. That is, effective paralanguage is perceived as an expression of interest, not an interruption.

Listening: This is the ability to not only to "hear", which is a physical attribute, but to also to be able to dedicate attentive and evaluative capabilities to an interaction.

CHAPTER 5

MOST FREQUENTLY REQUESTED COMMUNICATION STYLES

O ver the years we have heard many different style words suggested. Some were unique to the culture or setting in which they would be experienced. Some were reflective of a desired change in personality or lifestyle. In every case, remember, communication style coaching is a learning experience designed for those in a managerial or leadership position significant enough to have direct reports and a measurable impact on the organization. CSC is intended for those folks whose very presence in a room, in a meeting, has an effect on others. As such, each style word that is ultimately selected is as direct result of discussion, dissection, and sometimes debate between the client and the coach. All this is to ensure that the chosen words are understood equally by both parties. In some cases, this has produced style words that are rarely, if ever, duplicated by another person.

In this chapter we will review the style words that are most frequently selected by managers and leaders from around the globe and in a wide variety of businesses and industries. While it is true that each person has his or her own interpretation of these words, the following descriptions offer a starting point for customization. As we review each of these most frequently selected style words, note that each is modified by the sixteen variables that create a personal communication style. Be sure to go back to chapter 4 for a clear understanding of each of the sixteen variables as applied to the particular style word. Those variables will remain the same, but their applications will change with each different word. You will also note that the discussion of each style word is accompanied by a gender alert to provide additional insight into the application of the word.

Approachable: *Approachable* people give the impression of someone who would be kind, respectful and receptive if another person approached them. They do not appear standoffish or aloof, but friendly, open, and safe.

Approachable Communication Techniques:

Body language: A slower movement style. Standing, walking, or turning, soft sitting, not stiff or overly erect, is best. Standing in a business setting should be casual with one leg about six inches in front of the other, not crossed at the ankles. Slower movements of two or three steps are more desirable than pacing back and forth or standing still and swaying.

Gestures: Hand and arm gestures should be above the waist, hands open, not clenched. Pointing or referencing should be done by more than one finger to avoid an accusatory interpretation. Hands in pocket should be used occasionally to convey a relaxed impression. Arms should not be folded across the body. If they are crossed, be sure it is for short periods of time, no longer than thirty seconds each time. Handshakes should be offered proactively. The grasp should be firm but not to the point of squeezing.

Facial expressions: Eye contact should be into the face of others. Be sure not to stare, however. It is normal to move eye contact when speaking. When listening, it is also normal to look at the other person. Do not stare, however. It is normal to break eye contact every twenty to thirty seconds for five seconds. Smiling is very valuable for this word. A smile should not be given only when something is humorous. Approachable is a style word that requires a lot of smiling. Smiling with lips alone may not show a normal expression. Experiment in a mirror to find the smile you like best.

Vocal variety: Try to match the patterns of your listener. If he or she has a wide variety in their sound, then match it. If he or she has a more subdued speaking style, then match that. Do not mirror his or her style. That is, do not do exactly as he or she does. Merely show a similar level of vocal variety in your style to indicate that you are in tune with his or her level of concern.

Voice and speech: A softer volume is better than louder. Speaking should be natural. That is, do not give special emphasis to words that you think will impress. Use your most comfortable vocabulary. To the extent possible, use vocabulary and sentence structures that match those of your listener.

Color words: These should sync with your vocal variety, but do not use more colorful words than those being used by your listeners. Keep your color words in the same genre.

Articulation and pronunciation: Be yourself. Do not try to over articulate sounds. Absolutely do not try to match the accent of your listener. Use your normal articulation and pronunciation, of course. It is always advisable to speak clearly and not to mumble.

Rate and pace: Here are two more areas where the ability to match your listener will be helpful. The other person will find you more approachable and they can easily get in sync with your delivery.

Ethos, pathos, and logos: This is basically a pathos style. Each of the previously mentioned variables should be approached with a pathos mindset. The overall impression is one of a relaxed, self-confident person. An approachable person asks more questions than he or she makes statements, showing friendly interest in the others. Logos is used when the content calls for it and not randomly. Ethos of some sort (i.e. human or personal), will come as others feel the sense of sincerity and willingness to interact.

Language: Your vocabulary should be more informal than formal. Do not be overly concerned about precise sentence structuring. While it is important to be grammatically correct, it is not desirable to be so precise that it may sound out of sync with the surroundings. Choose words that seem to fit the level of comfort others exhibit.

Paralanguage: The type, intensity and frequency should follow the principle that less is more. Others need to feel assured that you will allow them to initiate and participate in interactions without interruption. Make good eye contact, but don't stare. Give the other person a break from your eye contact. Every thirty seconds or so, look away for three or four seconds. Nod occasionally. Use affirming paralanguage like, "I see," "How interesting," or if you want to be more informal, "I'll be darned," and "No kidding." You may also use your own paralanguage appropriate to the other person's style. Remember to be authentic. Don't say or do things just because the other person is doing them. Never use paralanguage that is more than three words. It will be perceived as an interruption rather than an affirmation of attention and approachability.

Listening: Make good eye contact, especially when you are being approached. During the dialogue be sure to continue eye contact, use soft paralanguage, such as, "Oh,", "I see,", and "Interesting.".

Approachable Gender Alerts

Overall, females smile more than males. Smiling is the key ingredient to signaling the style word *approachable*. In addition to smiling less, men use fewer facial expressions overall, perhaps making them harder to read. Certain professions, such as researchers and scientists, embody a dispassionate, clinical attitude through minimal facial expression. We have noted that in these fields, males and females can come across as equally unapproachable. A less-than-friendly demeanor can be problematic when old skills are used in a new role. Such was the case with Dr. Bob, an older physician. Dr. Bob shared that he was trained not to show too much expression when talking to a patient. (Thankfully, many medical schools these days teach the opposite, as recent research confirms how important a role facial expressions play in the physician-patient relationship.) As the new head of a biotech firm, Bob wanted to learn how to come across as more approachable. In addition to dumping the dull expressions, Bob worked on conveying approachability by telling a lighthearted anecdote when he opened a meeting and bringing in the donuts and coffee himself to staff meetings.

Though a phony smile can be often be detected since the usual smile muscles are not all engaged, we still encourage clients to fake it if they don't feel it. All indications are that when you use positive, friendly facial expressions, you will both convey that attitude to others and develop it in yourself. At least colleagues and clients will sense good intentions.

Women who lack the smile gene are more penalized than deficient males, since listeners may expect friendlier females. Lydia was the head administrator in charge of the fifty staff members in a large Boston law firm. Lydia knew that her staff found her unfriendly, which she blamed on the fact that she was too busy to say hello and make small talk. Lydia turned out to be one of our fastest learners. During our first meeting we advised her put on a smile and widen her eyes to convey the feeling of being *approachable*.

Authoritative: This communication style is not the same as *authoritarian*— the heavy-handed style that says, "my way or the highway." An *authoritative* person is someone who other people feel they can come to with a concern or problem and the *authoritative* person will either solve or provide guidance to solving the problem. In any case, the time spent interacting with an *authoritative* person always feels beneficial and productive.

The *authoritative* style is particularly interesting because it can be blended with nearly every other style. Being an authority on a subject does not preclude the ability to also be *personable* or *approachable*. However, in some cases, an *authoritative* person may not seem very *approachable* or even *personable*. To give others the impression of being *authoritative*, a person must exhibit both content and process knowledge. That is, he or she must be knowledgeable on the subject at hand, and must possess the communication skills to transfer that knowledge to others. This style word tends to be one of the most popular. This stands to reason when you realize that most people who go through communication style coaching are either in positions of leadership or are on the way there. It must be remembered that the techniques identified here are blended with the accompanying communication techniques ascribed to the other style word that has been chosen. Clients must choose two style words, as was noted earlier. Presenting oneself as *authoritative* can be a real asset. The question is, how does a person project an *authoritative* style? The answer is the ability to use these communication techniques.

Authoritative Communication Techniques

Body language: The movements are more deliberate. There is no unnecessary movement. While relaxed, even slouchy at times, movement is a bit slower and more reflective and responsive than self-motivated. Posture is casual, not rigid. Effort is made not to seem overbearing or suspicious to the other person.

Gestures: These are connected to the content a bit more than other style words. Hand and arm gestures are used to support, clarify, or emphasize points being made. Keep gestures above the waist and in front of you.

Facial expressions: Attention is given to produce expressions that are supportive of the person with whom you are speaking. Eye contact is generally maintained while listening. Don't stare. Do break eye contact periodically for about five to ten seconds. Smiling should be used to show empathy or understanding.

Vocal variety: It is not necessary to vary your vocal techniques very much. Stay within your normal range even if the other person uses a wide variety of vocal techniques. Your steadiness will communicate confidence and strength of communication.

Color words: Choose a few and repeat them periodically. Add color in light doses. Being too colorful will create suspicion that you may be hiding something.

Rate and pace: Keep these consistent without being too repetitive. That is, do not depend on these techniques to emphasize points. Your consistency will communicate confidence and comfort with your knowledge of the content.

Articulation and pronunciation: The clearer the better. Clear and accurate articulation and pronunciation will communicate an understanding of the content and evoke acceptance and confidence.

Voice and speech: Speak in lower tones than higher. Use your normal indoor voice and project as if your listener is six feet away. Speak in complete declarative sentences most of the time. Ask questions to show interest and mainly to gain information. Sound more like a teacher and teller than a probing seller.

Ethos, pathos, and logos: The very nature of the style word *authoritative* lends itself more to logos. Try adding pathos to your logos by smiling, using your listener's name, or sharing a personal anecdote.

Language: Keep it simple. Do not attempt to show how knowledgeable you are by using unusual words. Keep sentence structure simple. Shorter sentences will indicate an ability to make complex information easier to understand.

Paralanguage: Use it. Prepare a few key words, phrases, or sentences to use while you are listening. Remember, none of these should be longer than three words. Use soft volume when you use these. Sound strong and understanding.

Listening: Listening is important to this Style Word because you want to be perceived as paying attention to others. An Authoritative person does not look away while the other person is speaking. Don't stare, of course. You must look at the speaker more than you look away from the speaker. Avoid judgmental Paralanguage that may give an erroneous impression. Nodding, affirming comments are appropriate. They should indicate that you understand— not necessarily that you agree with the speaker. Ask questions to show interest and to gain the knowledge you need to give an Authoritative reply.

Authoritative Gender Alerts

Ask anyone which is the more authoritative sex, and nine out of ten responders will answer men. Though men and women are, of course, equally knowledgeable, men may be thought of as more authoritative for these key reasons:

- Men hold most of the highest positions in organizations—with women occupying less than 3 percent of the top spots but close to 50 percent of the workforce. These enduring trends have two consequences: certain traits, based on traditionally male behavior, are associated with authoritative, and females who choose authoritative as a style word may be judged by this male standard.
- Men are bigger and taller. Fair or not, we associate physical strength and height with leadership. Fortune 500 CEOs are, on average, six feet tall, or one and a half inches taller than the average male, and

30 percent are six foot two or more. The average American woman is less than five feet four inches. That means lots of looking up and plenty of high heels for the female leader.

- Men's lower-pitched voices are associated with authority.
- Male communicators may be more skilled at being direct, getting to the point, and offering advice.
- Females often demonstrate relationship smoothers such as being polite, good listening, and easing in to a situation to reduce an appearance of being abrupt, rude, or overbearing.
- Female clients in male-dominated fields like engineering, accounting, and science are often befuddled by how different they feel in a group of men. They ask what they need to do to be taken seriously. It is frustrating to *be* an expert, but not to be *acknowledged* as such.

Here are the five key behaviors for women who choose *authoritative* as a style word:

1. Communicate strategically. Increase how frequently you speak at meetings. Initiate one-on-one networking with individuals who can influence your career.

2. Take up space—be seen. One advantage you have if you are one of the few women at the meeting, you will be noticed. So, be noticed for your *authoritative* demeanor. Sit in a prime spot at meetings, in the center or the head of the table. Stand up when you can for a presentation. Keep your chair high and your arms out. Wear that strong and serious black or navy jacket, along with a sharp accessory. Audrey, financial analyst and my client of many years, often cites the impact of taking up space in her meetings with aggressive men. She was sold on the value of style coaching after just one meeting where, as she described it, the guys "actually listened to me."

3. Keep it short. Keep your main point to fifteen words or less. The head of the Tuck Business School at Dartmouth College described a leader as a person who "has a theme and repeats it frequently."

4. Use evidence and editorials. My smart female clients have been per-
    ceived as wishy-washy or soft. Beef up your content by building your
    case with data, facts, and charts. Don't stop there, ladies. Always
    integrate your facts with your expert opinion by offering a recom-
    mendation, opinion, or perspective.
5. Know what authoritative *sounds* like. Keep your voice at the low to
    middle range of your pitch. Convey impact through vocal variety,
    watching out for two pitch glitches: getting too high pitched when
    enthused, or using an upward inflection at the *end* of sentences.

Of course, these same guidelines are useful for men who want to be seen
as more *authoritative*. In addition, as an *authoritative* male in the new millen-
nium, watch out for confusing *authoritative* with *authoritarian*—coming on
too strong, loud, overbearing and blunt. Though in the short run, your team
may comply, bullying just leads to poor morale and sabotages productivity.

Enthusiastic: This style exudes energy. There seems to be an ever-
present sense of excitement and joy. An enthusiastic person is almost always
positive about issues, and can hardly wait to get started with the under-
taking. This style should not be mistaken for that overly energetic, in-your-
face person, like the Energizer bunny, who needs to try decaf a bit more.
Enthusiastic communicators usually show a good deal of smiling. They seem
always ready to get into action.

Enthusiastic Communication Techniques

Body language: There is a constant sense of readiness indicated by
more standing than sitting, more physical movement than motionless.
Movements can be small and slow. Movements, as relates to size, can be as
big as feels comfortable and appropriate to the setting and topic.

Gestures: Moving your hands and arms is a staple for this style. Hand
gestures are particularly important in communicating enthusiasm. They

should be palm open, facing your listener. Do not make a fist unless to express excitement, such as a fist pump. It is better to point with fingers closed and palm open. Thumbs up is also useful to indicate enthusiasm.

Facial expressions: This may be the most important nonverbal communication technique. Of course, smiling is a basic for showing enthusiasm. Laughing, on the other hand, can seem insincere. Use it sparingly. Eyes should be opened wide without looking shocked. Practice this in the mirror. Eye contact with your listener is important. Maintain it while the other person is speaking as well as when you begin and end your response.

Vocal variety: This communication technique is frequently used to show enthusiasm. It can be in the form of slightly increased volume, or a raised pitch on key words in the thought. Try to match these particular techniques with facial expressions to double the message of enthusiasm.

Color words: As with vocal variety, the very nature and purpose of color words is to show emotions such as enthusiasm. Listen carefully to the words your listener is using. Select the most meaningful ones and color those when you speak. The perfect blend to create the *enthusiastic* impression is a combination of emphasized color words spoken with vocal variety and a matching facial expression. To discover your comfort level in melding these three for a natural look and sound, practice with a mirror, video camera, or the camera on your phone until you find your comfort zone.

Rate and pace: Speed is dependent on the situation, although faster is better than slower to show enthusiasm. Slightly increased speed (both rate and pace) is appropriate. Refrain from interrupting, but initiate your responses within three seconds of the other person's conclusion.

Voice and speech: Use your normal voice except when the technique of vocal variety is utilized. Your voice may automatically rise in pitch when sounding enthusiastic, this is appropriate.

Ethos, pathos, and logos: The word *enthusiastic* is a pathos word. Exhibiting the techniques described in vocal variety, color words, and facial expression will create a pathos impression. When you are presenting logos material, be sure to decrease these pathos techniques by at least one half. If you have low ethos in the relationship it will be important not to be overly zealous in using these pathos techniques. It will make you look nervous and too eager to please. If you believe that low ethos is part of the perception others may have of you, be sure to cut the use of pathos techniques by one half except at the beginning and the end of the interactions. At these times you want to seem happy to be entering the interaction and glad to have been part of it at the end.

Paralanguage: It is helpful to use this technique frequently during the interaction. It will help to give the sense of enthusiasm for being part of the interaction.

Keep your paralanguage to three words or fewer so as to avoid the impression of interrupting. Use an up inflection with paralanguage that is not in the form of words such as, "mmm," "ahh," or "ooh." Match your paralanguage with your facial expression whenever possible.

Listening: While the other person is speaking you can use affirming paralanguage that shows your reaction to the comments being made. If your reaction is happy, show that. If your reaction is surprise, show that, etc.. When you respond to the speaker, do so with a little silence before you begin speaking. The intent is to show your eagerness to share thoughts without interrupting or over powering the other person. Smiling is a good use of Paralanguage for this Style Word.

Enthusiastic Gender Alerts

Women are more likely than men to convey enthusiasm in the amount of smiling, range of facial expressions, and quantity of vocal variety and gestures. Nothing wrong with that, but, women need to keep in mind that you should match your displays of enthusiasm by demonstrating authority and competence, lest you get crowned with the cheerleader label.

Sarah Palin is a famous example of someone who has enthusiasm, conveyed not only in her communication style, but also in her lifestyle (think ice fishing, hunting, and dog sledding). These traits make her a sought-after speaker and the recipient of plenty of invitations to host talk shows. Yet, her great enthusiasm, combined with good looks, overshadows her displays of political knowledge and intelligence, leading many in both parties to consider her a bit too bubbly for a presidential run.

So, unless you are running your own company, ladies, do not let your positive energy dampen your reputation as a serious player. Though clients of both sexes often choose enthusiasm as a style word, I've noted that women are penalized more than men for being serious or dull. Some male professionals are fearful of seeming too enthusiastic, and I have to reassure them that though they won't turn into Richard Simmons, perhaps they'll end up a fraction as motivating as he is.

Liam, an engineer by training, was viewed as a potential CEO of a heavy equipment firm, if only he could come across as more inspiring. Fortunately he was a motivated client, though it seemed like learning how to convey enthusiasm was as challenging as learning a new language. Liam's new style was unveiled when he led the annual company retreat. Our coaching on using more examples and interaction to inspire a range of facial expressions, standing near the group rather than at the screen, and knowing his content well enough to enhance his speed, fluency, and vocal variety, really paid off.

Women have one vocal advantage—they habitually use a wider pitch range for expressiveness.

However, many male clients need a push to show vocal *enthusiasm* through vocal variety and color words. One low-key client, Fred, a leader of a biotech company, was referred to us because he did not seem passionate enough about his work. Fred shared that in his former role as a medical lab director, his style worked great with scientists. Now, it was putting his leadership team to sleep. It did take Fred a few coaching sessions to both be willing to even try the vocal techniques for enthusiasm, and to feel that he didn't look foolish using them. Eventually, with practice and careful use of the techniques at home and then at work, Fred realized how differently his colleagues perceived him when he exhibited the more enthusiastic style.

Confident: This word can be understood to mean showing confidence or instilling confidence. Both are viable. Here we will emphasize the intent of showing confidence. We recognize the value in being able to build confidence in others. We also acknowledge creating the feeling of confidence within oneself. These qualities and competencies are indeed admirable. They would normally contribute to creating a *confident* impression in the marketplace. However, here we will focus on those communication techniques that project an air of self-confidence to others. As with all style words, the techniques suggested must be factored into the circumstances of the particular situation and interaction. With this word, extra care must be taken not to appear overconfident, cocky, or arrogant. This style is communicated in subtle ways. Each of the following techniques should be practiced before being introduced into meaningful interactions.

Confident Communication Techniques

Body language: No swaggering. No chest thumping. Confidence is displayed in subtle ways in everyday life. While swaggering and chest thumping may be appropriate for sports, they are the antithesis of day-to-day displays of confidence. Generally, less movement is better than more. That is, make moves that have a beginning and an end. Leg crossing, for instance, should happen all in one motion. Tightly crossed legs look more confident than legs crossed with the ankle balanced on the opposite knee. When walking, your strides should be evenly spaced and the speed (appropriate to the situation) should be consistent, giving the impression of decisiveness.

Gestures: Confident gestures are closer to the body in small spaces and further from the body in large spaces. Open hand gestures should be made palms facing toward the body. Avoid pointing at others. If fingers are used to number the points being made, each finger should relate to a single point. Do not hang one finger on another.

Facial expressions: These should be more restrained than expressive. Smiling should be somewhat less than your maximum ability. Smile slightly when delivering sentences that could be perceived as offensive. Be careful not to smirk at these times. In order to be sure you are in control of your smile, here is an exercise designed to give you control over the muscles that control your smile. This is a muscle memory exercise. Practice this in the mirror this way: Begin with no smile. Very slowly create a closed-lip smile. Very slowly show teeth. Very slowly expose many teeth with your widest smile. Very slowly reverse this exercise. This should take approximately thirty seconds. Look for the most acceptable smile and remember how it feels. Finally, try to create it without a mirror. Reach for the same feeling. Now look in the mirror to see if it looks the way you want it to be. Maintain eye contact through an entire sentence. Then hold it for about three more seconds.

Vocal variety: This can go two ways depending on your personality. If you are an outgoing person who finds it easy to contribute to a conversation, you may also find it easy to vary your voice. You may use high and low pitch frequencies. You may raise and lower your volume to express your ideas. If, on the other hand, you are a quieter personality who does not feel comfortable being loud or assertive in a conversation, you may find it more satisfying to keep your vocal variety fairly steady. On balance, a more steady and normal use of vocal change will express more confidence. Know yourself and choose wisely.

Voice and speech: A *confident* style can follow the same coaching found in the previous paragraph about vocal variety. Depending on which type of personality you have, these techniques can go either way. First decide whether you are more extraverted or more introverted as a personality, then choose according to the coaching in the previous paragraph. Although, we are adding the characteristic of speech, the coaching is very similar. To be more specific, see the following paragraphs on color words, rate, and pace.

Color words: The most important caution here is not to be too colorful. Use color words to emphasize main thoughts and key words. It is not necessary to find color words in every sentence. It is important to know exactly which words do the most for understanding, clarity, or persuasion. Those are the ones to color.

Rate and pace: This is not a situation where slow and steady wins the race, but it is important to be consistent. Do not vary either of these too much. That is, vary these because the idea calls for it, not just because you can do it. It is important to show confidence in your thinking as expressed in these speeds of speaking.

Articulation and pronunciation: You will not seem *confident* if these two are sloppy or careless. Naturally, there are exceptions to this. In fact, there may be situations where to be too articulate may be detrimental to your success. It may actually be more beneficial to be a bit carefully careless with your speech. Such moments can be critical in making a point. However, on the whole, you will give a more *confident* impression if others are able to clearly understand and admire you for your careful production of words.

Ethos, pathos, and logos: Confident communicators are able to use all three of these. Their use will depend on the situation, of course. To appear *and* feel the most confident, most speakers report that when they can combine solid logos with meaningful pathos that will lead them to ethos. So, as you organize your thoughts and begin to express them, start with logos, move to pathos, and allow that structure to build your ethos.

Paralanguage: Less is more. That's the general behavior pattern for a *confident* person. He or she possesses little or no need to augment his or her speaking with paralanguage. However, a confident speaker also shows appropriate, small paralanguage when listening. It shows the speaker that what he or she is saying is important. Head nods, "uh-huhs," and other simple two-word paralanguage utterances will help to show that you are confident enough in your own thoughts that you can give careful attention to other speakers.

Listening: Paralanguage is an important part of effective listening with most Style Words. It is particularly helpful here. Make consistent eye contact. Avoid constant eye contact. That will feel like you are staring. Look away for no more than three3 seconds when you do break eye contact. Ask closed specific ended questions. They sound more like you understand and are confident of your thought processing. You can also respond with comments like, "I understand" and "very interesting.". Do not interrupt the other person. Do comment, when appropriate, with direct language and word choice.

Confident Gender Alerts

Women, more than men, need to demonstrate confidence by taking up more physical space. Females are vertically disadvantaged, since people associate presence with height and strength.

The best stance for a woman who wants to be seen as confident is to spread out at a meeting, lean twenty degrees forward, and if she's not the tallest, make sure she sits in the tall chair. A good stance for a female includes set apart at shoulder width, gestures above the waist and six inches or more from her sides. The good news, even for the most petite, is these behaviors *can* compensate for small stature. I like the word *bantam*—small but mighty!

(Men need to be aware of the power of physical space, and to be seated if a more equal relationship is desired. Conversely, if you tower over others, it is nature's gift to you for a confident presence. Studies in *Social Science Quarterly* revealed that people prefer business and political leaders to be taller and more physically imposing. Watch out though for stances that signal arrogance, such as leaning back, or putting your hands on your hips with your elbows out. Shorter guys need not despair—your competence and overall style matters way more that your height. You will though, need to compensate with a strong voice and the ability to use authoritative language when it makes sense to seem in control.)

In order to be perceived as confident, women need to *sound* confident. Males have a naturally lower optimum or best pitch and that pitch range is associated with presence and confidence. I work with many of my female clients to help them find a lower pitch level that is still comfortable. Additionally, many women have a thin voice, a leftover from their teen years, which sounds way too girlish for a grownup. They laugh when I advise adding calories to their vocal tone, making it richer and more resonant. (Think Oprah.) Women (and some unsure males too) need to make sure they control "uptalk"—an upward inflection, or rising tone at the end of a declarative sentence. Such uptalk will be perceived as unsure or overly acquiescent.

(Both males and females need to make sure that volume is maintained through the end of a thought, and that the voice can project to the person farthest away in the meeting room. A male manager I work with is perceived as unsure. He begins thoughts with appropriate volume, but then becomes soft and mumbling mid sentence. Males with booming baritones may consciously need to soften their voices in order to project the right level of self-assurance. Too loud and strong signals an attempt at dominance, not real confidence.)

Motivational: This is an interesting style. It is also a very popular style word. Naturally, most people who are in leadership positions want to, in fact need to, motivate others. The basic idea behind being *motivational* is that you are able to get others to do what you want them to do. There are many books been written about how to be motivational. As with all style word coaching, if you choose a path that involves human-to-human interaction, the following communication techniques will be very valuable. There are two important points to be made about *motivational*.

First of all, it is important to note that you cannot ever motivate a person to do anything. Each person must decide to do whatever it is on his or her own. What you can do is to create the mind-set and environment surrounding the individual that in turn helps them to motivate themselves and complete the task.

Second, there is a significant difference between the word *motivational* and the word *inspirational*. Many people equate the two. They are different. An *inspirational* speaker is one who can touch the emotions of listeners. Listeners are able to get excited about the speaker's subject. The listener feels a rising passion about the subject. This is often what we find with religious preachers. The faithful get excited and emotional for the subject. The preacher is able to inspire thoughts in some emotional direction, but that's it. An inspirational speaker will tap into the emotions of the listeners, but then leaves it to them to take the next step. Sometimes, the next step is obvious. Often it is not. The next step is left to the decision of the listener. The next step may be quite different to each listener. But, each has been inspired.

A *motivational* speaker is similar to an *inspirational* speaker, but is different in one important way. The difference is that a *motivational* speaker does not leave the decision as what the next action should be to the listener. A *motivational* speaker gives the listener a specific action to take. A *motivational* speaker gives the listener something to do with the emotions that have been aroused. This is the big difference between a *motivational* and an *inspirational* speaker.

Motivational Communication Techniques

Vocal variety: There is almost no way to say exactly what are the best vocal techniques to create the word *motivational*. In many ways, motivation is in the ear of the listener. Perhaps the best vocal technique is to ensure that you don't sound like you are trying to motivate someone. Different situations, different listeners, different topics, different times of day, different locations, and so on will all influence the choice of appropriate vocal techniques to be used. Actually, in some cases it will be important to add little or no variety to the sound of your voice. It will be the sound of familiarity and normalcy that will help motivate. Assess the listener, the topic, and your purpose, only then choosing the appropriate vocal technique.

Color words: Your words should be chosen according to what you feel will move the listener. They may not be the words that would move or motivate you. It's not about you. What specific words will be most influential in the listener's world? Those are the words to color. They may be nouns, pronouns, adjectives, or adverbs. There is no grammatical right or wrong here. Choose words that are related to the action or feeling you are trying to create. If it's a particular action, use action-oriented words. If it is a feeling or belief, use words that you believe will resonate with the listener on a more emotional level. Be yourself. Speak like yourself. Don't be shy about giving extra strength to words that you know will be meaningful to your listener.

Articulation and pronunciation: These two techniques are always important to promote clarity. However, you do not need to be extra cautious when articulating and pronouncing words unless those words are key to the thought of motivation. Remember, you are creating a mind-set and an environment. Sometimes those environments are best constructed by a bit of sloppy articulation. I can hardly believe I just said that! But it is true that listeners respond to the sound of the speaker to tell whether they can relate. Your listener is evaluating whether you have the clarity that I need to feel compelled to do what is asked of me? On the other hand, do not try to create the local or regional accent of your listener. That can be insulting.

Rate and pace: Remember, these two characteristics of speaking style relate to speed. They are particularly valuable when trying to motivate people. Generally speaking, it is better to speak at a faster rate and pace when attempting to motivate. It's not a race. You don't have to be faster than everyone else. When you increase your rate of speech words, it will show your excitement about the subject. Listeners will tend to follow that excitement. Your pace, or the speed of your thoughts, on the other hand, must be delivered according to the listeners' ability to understand the subject. Vary the pace to emphasize particular points. Be careful not to fall into a repeated pattern of rate and pace, however. That would seem rehearsed, boring, and the opposite of *motivational*.

Body language: Here you need a mix of intense and controlled. It may seem that to motivate another person that you need to be a ranting, charging, in-your-face, and hyperbolic speaker. Not true. Yes, it is helpful to show your excitement for the subject with hand, arm, and body movement. The issue is, of course, how much. Depending on the setting, less is more. The old image of a football coach may not be at all helpful in settings other than football. Stand straight, as tall as you can. Hold your head up. These will show control and determination. It may also be helpful, on the other hand, to bend or lean to indicate intensity of feeling.

Facial expressions: Your expressions should match the emotion or action you are trying to motivate in the other person. Joy, happiness, and the like should be accompanied by smiling, laughing, and the like. A more serious intent should be accompanied by a more serious look. Lips more closed than open. Eyes with little movement. It is very important that you are in control of these expressions. Too often we see and hear a speaker whose message in words is positive, but whose facial expression is negative. The face is, perhaps, the most frequent offender of sending mixed messages. Learn to feel your face. That is, practice how much movement it takes for you to express a given message.

Gestures: Hand and arm movements can actually be a bit scary to listeners if not controlled and used in sync with the message being delivered. Similar to facial expressions, speakers are often saying one thing but showing something different by the way they gesture with hands and arms.

Generally, big statements can be accompanied by big movement. Smaller, words and thoughts and images should be accompanied by smaller gestures. Motivating others is both a mental and physical effort. If thoughts and words are not supported by appropriate gestures, you are sending mixed messages, and *motivation* will not happen.

Voice and speech: These can be very powerful in motivating others. Each motivational situation will be different, so you must be flexible in your use of both your voice and your speech. Generally speaking, your voice is most effective at either end of your range. That is, soft or loud. When you are at the point in your speaking when you will say what you believe will be most *motivational*, choose to use either end of your vocal range. The idea is to use your voice in a slightly different way when you are actually saying the words that you believe are *motivational*. The same is true with your speech. When you speak the words that you believe will be most *motivational*, use your color words. Vary your articulation and pronunciation. Be a bit more articulate, perhaps, or a bit faster or slower, perhaps, or put a bit more or less emphasis on a particular sound in a word, perhaps. Your voice and speech are the end of the process of being *motivational*. You must first be completely certain of what you believe is the most *motivational* thing you have to say in a particular setting.

Ethos, pathos, and logos: Choosing which of these is most appropriate to your purpose and listeners can be a daunting task. People can be motivated by any of these. If you are to be a *motivational* communicator, you must have good control over each of these. I cannot tell you which is going to work every time with which type of listener or topic or setting. The truth is that *you* cannot motivate anyone. *You* cannot make someone do something or believe something. You can create the environment in which they want to do or believe something. You can use ethos, pathos, and logos to both create that environment and to fill it with the appropriate ethos, pathos, or logos thoughts or data. That is, you can do that, *if* you are clear on your intention, the wants and needs of your listeners, and your desired outcome.

Paralanguage: This is a powerful variable when attempting to motivate people. In addition to the appropriate words and language, the way you look is critical. Smile as much as is appropriate. Offer positive affirmations to the other person, showing your belief in his or her thinking and abilities. Lean toward the other person. Use all your gestures to express your belief in the conversation and the ideas being shared. Nod in agreement whenever possible.

Listening: Make good eye contact. Ask questions that have a positive tenor to them. That is, without interrupting, when appropriate, ask a question based on your listening, that will elicit a positive response. Use paraphrasing to reinforce positive thinking.

Motivational Gender Alerts

The behaviors we use to motivate and the style we best respond to can be strongly influenced by our gender.

It helps to consider the following: How is the way I motivate influenced by gender? How do I adjust my style depending on whether I am talking to a man or woman?

Let's look at a couple of recent clients who needed to consider these questions.

Robyn, an attractive, well-dressed analyst in the commercial real estate field, was promoted to sales manager, leading a group of ten young men. Her male manager referred her because she was boring and uninspiring, especially in a group. My client realized that she had been comfortable hanging with the guys in the past and wondered why her style wasn't working in her new leadership role.

Robyn and other women need to be aware of motivating by doing these things: Maintaining at least a moderate level of vocal and facial-expression variety. Avoiding toning down the emotions so much that you appear emotionless. Using language that speaks to benefits and results. Using I and we statements to avoid seeming demanding or whining. Avoiding tentative language or qualifiers.

Ed, a partner in a management consulting firm, called me to say that his assistant and other women on his team found him loud and unapproachable. Ed declared that if his team didn't know the right thing to do, it was his right to just tell them. Come on guys, unless you *are* a three-star general, drop the military demeanor in favor of a more inclusive *motivational* style. Ed and other men need to do the following: Build the case, not tell people what to do. Incorporate pathos-building tactics such as inviting comments, criticism, and suggestions. Facilitate a group discussion, using stories, examples and quotes.

If you are known for coming on strong, have the courage to try on this softener, especially when speaking to women: control your vocal tone to a moderate level of volume and vocal variety. You may get temporary buy-in with the loud voice and fist pounding, but you may see the troops going AWOL when the task is complete.

Comfortable: This person seems easy to be with and, most of all, seems at ease with him or herself. A person who has a *comfortable* communication style is a good listener, gives off nonthreatening impressions, seems interested in others, and is generally someone with whom it is easy to have interaction. Movements, vocabulary, and topics discussed all indicate a person who has self-confidence and comfort interacting with others. Even when upset or angry about something, this person does not show outward signs of aggression or despair. Others may often refer to this person as "very nice" or "laid back."

Comfortable Communication Techniques

Articulation and pronunciation: *Comfortable* should not be confused with sloppy. A comfortable style does not equate with being slovenly or mumbling. The clarity with which you produce language is very important to this communication style. It is very easy for a speaker to lapse into something sloppiness, thinking that it is not necessary to be articulate. If you are to also communicate a sense of competence and confidence, you must be articulate and pronounce your words clearly. In fact, that actually will give listeners an impression of comfort and confidence in your ability to communicate effectively.

Vocal variety: You will notice that when someone is very comfortable with those around them, they project a wide variety of vocal tones. When things are humorous, the voice may get higher or may imitate a perceived attitude. When they are sad, the voice reflects that. It often causes others to ask, "What's wrong?" The same is true when you desire to project a *comfortable* image. Vary your vocal pitch, volume, and intensity to suit your message and the mood of the group.

Voice and speech: Ask yourself what kind of voice and speech in other people makes you *un*comfortable? You certainly don't want to sound like that. Check your voice and speech by taping yourself, and by asking a trusted friend for personal feedback. Generally, softer is more comforting to others. Avoid shouting, unless it is to show excitement.

Color words: These are very important in projecting a comfortable image. It says that you are comfortable enough, secure enough, and confident enough to stress the main points in your thinking in a different manner than other thoughts. Use them to the degree that you are comfortable with them. But remember, you are developing and delivering this style for others to ascribe to you. Color words may feel a bit unusual to you, at first. You may have to practice this technique in safe places before using it in more important settings.

Facial expressions: Don't stare at people. It makes them uncomfortable and can make you seem too aggressive and not comfortable to be around. Of course, make eye contact when speaking to others. Move the eye contact away from the person with whom you are speaking approximately every fifteen seconds. I know that seems like a lot of looking away. However, when you break eye contact, do it for only three or four seconds. In addition, breaking away gives the listener a chance to freshen up. That is, he or she can blink, scratch his or her nose, yawn, stretch his or her facial muscles, or do a number of personal things. Don't make them uncomfortable by being too intense with your eye contact.

Body language: This is one of the most important communication techniques for this style word. Again, comfortable body language does not mean being sloppy or disrespectful of others. Become familiar with your body and the impression it makes in the space you share with others. Be respectful of the differences between social space (four to six feet), personal space (two to three feet), and intimate space (one foot or less). Never invade a person's personal space, and certainly not his or her intimate space. That is, don't stand or sit to close to them. Project relaxed and in control postures. Stand erect but not rigid. Sit comfortably without slouching and looking uninterested.

Gestures: Do not choreograph gestures. We could say the same thing about the previous two communication techniques, as well. A *comfortable* person will have gestures that are natural, not contrived, that are within his or her personality, and within the environs of the larger human setting. Importantly, the gestures will be considerate of the person who is listening to you, especially those close, say within three or four feet. Gestures will be smaller than larger. They will be softer than stronger. They will also be slower than faster.

Ethos, pathos, and logos: The very word *comfortable* indicates that the dominant mode will be pathos. This does not mean in any way that ethos and logos are not effective and persuasive. However, it does mean that you must be aware of any disconnect between what you say, how you say it, and how you look when you say it. This, obviously, includes the communication techniques identified earlier. It also includes body language, facial expressions, and gestures. Even when you are delivering a logos content, you should couch it in a more pathos technique. This may be exhibited in posture, hand gestures, and rate and pace of speaking, to note a few. It is even helpful to analyze your dress style to see if your clothing projects a *comfortable* style. Be sure not to confuse *comfortable* with *casual* or *carefree*. Ladies and gentlemen can be quite comfortable in a suit, if that is appropriate.

Paralanguage: This is one of the best-kept secrets of the effective *comfortable* communication style. Using *comfortable* paralanguage definitely helps others see and feel your sense of self-confidence and comfort. Use of paralanguage should be subtle. That is, it should be within your vocal range, your normal volume range, and typical of your body language, facial expressions, and gestures. It is important to use paralanguage. If you do not, you can both seem tense and cause others to feel uncomfortable with or for you. This, then, can lead to them not trusting you.

Listening: Be sure to give those signals that indicate that you are paying attention. Make eye contact. Ask easy questions. Paraphrase slowly. Use words and language that match those of the other person.

Comfortable Gender Alerts

A comfortable style needs to be viewed by both sexes in the context of what might be perceived as *too* comfortable for a positive business and professional image. Men and women alike need to realize they are always working when in a professional role. Though it's tempting, fun, and authentic to come across as comfortable, there may be a price to pay.

A few thoughts come to mind.

Differentiate comfortable from sloppy or sleazy. A female VP felt like dressing for the company theme party at a local zoo. She wore a leather jacket and a leopard-patterned miniskirt, which her male colleagues remembered, well, forever! No wonder she was referred to me for work on building her credibility.

Recently, I coached Max, the male CEO of a large industrial supply company. My visits were always on Fridays, coinciding with the company's casual day. His executive assistant teased me for overdressing in my pantsuit, as she happily wore a sweatshirt and jeans. Though I promised her I'd look more informal next time, I knew sweats would not be the way to go for making a professional impression, casual day or not!

Many men love losing the formal look, especially when it involves that three-letter word, T-I-E. But make sure *comfortable* still involves a good fit and good quality. And no shorts, tee shirts, or sandals if you are doing business with those outside your circle of close colleagues.

Differentiate comfortable from too casual and personal. Female professionals may enjoy bonding at work with trusted coworkers. Many of us make treasured friendships at work—always a good thing. But ladies, watch out for being perceived as too needy or provocative when sharing with a male colleague.

Men, please remember that getting too comfortable in conversation with females who work *for* you is tempting but full of land mines.

Case in point: My well-intentioned client, Marcus, an educational administrator, developed a work friendship with his colleague Robyn. She confided all, including her gynecological test results, to him and he responded by showing interest. To make a long story short, I ended up accompanying him to HR mediations, as, much to his dismay, he had been accused of harassment.

Personable: This person is the type you have to get to know. While he or she may seem uncomfortable or aloof at the initial meeting, once you get to know him or her, the person may be quite nice and easy to be with. First impressions with this person can be less than exciting. A *personable* individual is not nasty and doesn't give off unpleasant vibes. The first impression may not be as memorable as with someone who is *approachable*, or *enthusiastic*, for instance. This communication style has its most impact when there is time and occasion to interact with others. Like the style *comfortable*, other people will tend to ascribe similar communication techniques and expectations to you. It is also worth noting that there is a difference between being *personable* and being personal. Being *personable* is a professional skill. It is made up of a series of learned behaviors and attitudes. Being *personable* does not mean that you must reveal personal information. It does not mean that you have to engage in intimate conversations. It does not mean that you have to discuss topics that have personal or private meaning to you. You may know people who are all too eager to tell you things about their personal lives that you really don't want to know. To those individuals it may not seem at all unusual or uncomfortable to discuss personal financial, medical, religious, or other normally private topics. In fact, it may be embarrassing to listen to them. Of course, each person has his or her own definition of personal or private. You will have to decide that for yourself. This style word, *personable*, is not like that. Personable is a style that allows others to feel that you are asking or sharing thoughts about topics that are not personal but about which you have some feeling. Personable feels nonthreatening. It feels safe to be around.

Personable Communication Techniques

Voice and speech: These two communication tools should not overwhelm those with you. Volume and tone should be soft, not harsh. Those around you in a small group should be able to hear you without straining. Do not be the loudest or the softest speaker in the group.

Vocal variety: Less is more. Yes, be yourself, but understand that others may not resonate with any kind of aggressive or in-your-face, type of interaction. While vocal variety is an essential tool for letting others know just how you feel about a subject, it will be easily misinterpreted if it is more than the other person displays. People like to be with people like themselves. Try to match the sound of your voice and the amount of variety to the person with whom you are interacting.

Articulation and pronunciation: Like so many other communication techniques, it is best to be yourself. Do not try to create an impression by over articulating words. If you normally speak in contractions, do that: use you're for you are and it's for it is. Of course, do be careful that your sound is not sloppy or careless. You may come across as unsophisticated or uneducated. If you are unsophisticated or uneducated, and are happy with that, then be yourself.

Color words: Using colorful words can be a distinctive trait of your *personable* style. That does not mean that you should use words that are obscene, vulgar, or insulting. It does mean that you are free to use words that give extra meaning to your intentions. It does mean that you can use words that reveal your perception and perspective on the subject. It does mean that you can be expressive and have opinions. However, do not overwhelm others with argumentative exchanges.

Rate and pace: Both of these are important to this style word. Choose a rate and pace of speaking that matches those around you. This does not mean that you have to be acting. It does mean that you should control the speed at which you speak to match that of others. Do not try to speak like them. That is, do not mirror or be an exact copy of others. Do try to match their speed. Try to be at about the same rate and pace as those around you. They will find you a person who is easy to talk to if they also find you easy to listen to.

Facial expression, body language, and gestures: These three communication techniques are grouped together for the style word *personable* because they all require the same type of attention and utilization. People tend to like being with people like them. So, as we just pointed out above, try to match, not mirror, the behaviors of those around you. This does not mean that you should not be comfortable. This does not mean that you should be doing things you wouldn't normally do. It does mean that, to the extent that you can, try to be comfortable with the same type of facial expressions, body language, and gestures that are used by the group you are in. It will help others see you as easy to get along with. It is important to note that you should never do anything that is beyond your personal code of conduct. Even if you could do it, you will eventually come off as phony and not trustworthy. For instance, touching someone's elbow is different than touching someone's leg. Putting your arm around someone's shoulder is different that putting your arm around someone's waist. Winking, despite how you may intend it, can easily be misunderstood. If you are at all in doubt as to whether it is appropriate or not, it probably isn't. Don't do it. Remember, being *personable* is not being personal.

Ethos, pathos, and logos: As with the style word *comfortable*, the word *personable* carries with it the aura of pathos. Being *personable* connotes being friendly and easy to get along with. Those are pathos characteristics. To use logos or ethos with this style word, it will be important to vary the other communication techniques slightly to avoid your thoughts being received in a strictly pathos manner. It's nice and *personable* to smile at folks, but if you are trying to make a logos point, it can easily be misunderstood. Be sure not to give mixed messages.

Paralanguage: Others will see you as *personable* if you make them feel at ease. That means smile, make eye contact, and face the person with whom you are communicating. The style word *approachable* can provide guidance here. Please refer to those comments.

Listening: Allow the other person to speak freely. Do not interrupt. However, it is important to show interest in their his or her comments. So, make eye contact. Show that you are paying attention by asking non chal-lenging questions that do not challenge. Make affirming remarks when appropriate. Paraphrase a bit more frequently than you normally would to show that you are interested in clearly understanding.

Personable Gender Alerts

Both sexes are wise to consider *personable* as a style choice. *Personable* is a perfect style word for female professionals, who are perceived most posi-tively when they don't lean either too friendly or cold and unapproachable.

Women have two advantages regarding *personable*. First, many wom-en have a heightened ability to read a situation and determine what level of exchange of feelings, thoughts and information will be most effective. Secondly, the communication signals for *personable*—smiling and a range of facial expressions—are highly approved of in most business contexts in western culture. (Grown women are still told to smile when they break the *personable* rule, which of course makes them want to growl instead.)

Tim and Teresa, computer industry vice-presidents, frequently went to high-profile clients for marketing meetings. Though Tim was knowledge-able and expressed himself kindly, his lack of facial expressions made him so difficult to read that clients would gravitate to Teresa, whose expressive face and somewhat louder voice enhanced client comfort from the get-go. Teresa also succeeded on the *personable* scale with her avid signals that she was listening—forward lean, expressive nods, and frequent affirmations like, "That's great to hear, Juan." However, Tim's impassivity was a bit ex-treme. He was a self-proclaimed geek who had focused more on technology than people, and he, like many males, lost relationship points for not placing value on demonstrating his personable side.

To perfect *personable*, women need to manage the degree of person-ability shown. When influencing other men and women, females should match the level of friendliness shown by their conversational partner, but not exceed by more than a half step in terms of vocal volume and facial expressions. It could feel overwhelming. Both genders should plan for personable versus personal topics prior to an important meeting. For example, discussing the benefits of visiting Europe or seeing America first is a *personable* topic. Sharing your view on immigration policy, which reflects on background and deep values, is too risky.

Female professionals can value the role that personability plays in building business relationships. One client, the head of a large administration team in a major law firm, thought she was supposed to be businesslike. Instead, she found that simply by smiling and saying hello versus walking hurriedly down the corridor, she was able to positively influence morale and productivity. Men need to elevate the importance of a personable demeanor by greeting others with enthusiasm, speaking with more facial expression, and engaging others in small talk to show interest.

Personability demonstrated in the right degree enhances comfort and trust, and may be as important as your expertise, knowledge, and skills.

CHAPTER 6
CLIENT COMMENTS ON COMMUNICATION STYLE COACHING

Earlier, in chapter 2, we mentioned the difference between personality and persona. Briefly, that is that the persona is the core, the vault, within which each of us holds the true and basic values on which we build those behaviors that become our personality. This is important because communication style coaching will have a very small chance of becoming successful or effective if it interferes with or counters those values held within the persona. Understanding this will help the selection of the style words that frame and direct the path of the learning. No matter how fervently a person wants to acquire a particular communication style, it will be very challenging for that communication style to be sustainable if it is not comfortably aligned with the core values held in the persona.

Choosing style words is not just a matter of wishing. Imagining who you would like to become may be a good start in the formulation of an effective and comfortable communication style, but the real value, authenticity, and effectiveness will come when the chosen style words are in sync with those core values held within the persona.

It is entirely possible that two individuals will choose the same style words, but use entirely different communication techniques to manifest that style. This is thanks to the differences in the variables that make each person different from each other person. Our years of experience combined with the ensuing learning and practice of communication style coaching enables us to describe the communication techniques and characteristics that are most generally related to and recognized as part of a particular communication style. It is this knowledge and experience that form the basis of our comments for this book.

With all these thoughts in mind, it will be helpful to hear the words of several people who have experienced communication style coaching. Within this disparate group you will notice several similar themes. Yet these individuals do not know each other. They come from a wide variety of backgrounds, businesses, and cultures. They reflect interactions with different coaches. What follows are their descriptions of what effect communication style coaching has had on them.

Carol is the president of a private research foundation that does the majority of its business in the burgeoning field of communication technology. Her work requires her to interact with both for-profit and not-for-profit groups as they assist governments in the formulation of legislation and regulation of this constantly evolving world of communication technology. Her expertise also places in front of congressional committees, regulators, and others whose decision-making processes depend on accurate information and interpretation of technical data. She interacts with both highly technical individuals as well as others who have little or no knowledge or understanding of the technologies with which they find themselves involved. Her effectiveness is needed in both interpersonal and public forums. The topics she deals with can be minute, highly technical, and very public. Her formal coaching interaction lasted approximately one year. Her periodic, refresher, and supportive coaching has lasted several years. She chose the style words *authoritative* and *persuasive*. This is her reaction to communication style coaching:

*"Communication style coaching has enabled me to both ex-
pand my understanding of the challenges that others have
with the complexities of my content and, more importantly,
how I must adjust my communication style and techniques
to reach the decision makers and influencers who hold the
keys to helping our nation avoid the disastrous consequences of not being able to communicate with each other during
large (and small) scale disasters. I am now able to communicate in simple enough and direct enough language and
organization that allows others to grasp the importance of
my message. The self-awareness and skill sets that I have
acquired have enabled me to organize, present and modify
my messages on the spot when needed, which is most of the
time in my world. I am eternally grateful for the opportunity
to learn and grow my professional and personal communication style."*

Charles is the director of sales training and management for a large international manufacturing company based in the Unites States with cites in
sixty-nine countries across the Americas, Asia, Australia, Europe, Africa and
the Middle East. His communication responsibilities require cross cultural as
well as native interactions. The complexities of his content are multiplied by
this challenge. Whether in direct contact or through managers and others
throughout the world, his communication must be both well organized and
clearly delivered. The degree to which others can understand and accept his
leadership is directly related to his ability to develop trusting relationships
that cut across cultural and proximity barriers. His formal coaching interaction lasted approximately eight months. His informal coaching has lasted
many years as reminders and refreshers due to changing life and work variables. His style words are *approachable* and *motivational*. This is his reaction
to communication style coaching:

*"I am required to travel a great deal in my work. This can pres-
ent a challenge in both professional and personal relationships.*

There are issues of continuity, relevancy, familiarity, trust, and authenticity to name a few communication challenges. My experience with communication style coaching has been nothing short of incredible in the way it has impacted my personal and professional lives. It has improved the quality of my life, especially in business. I am able to achieve business results that are beyond my own expectations. I eagerly guide my direct reports and friends to experience it. I like to think that I am the best example of how effective an impactful it can be in forming positive relationships that lead to productive results."

Mary is an accomplished author and sought-after speaker as an expert in the fields of healthcare and technology innovation. She was also a driving force behind the start-up of one of America's most influential technology research firms. As a recognized expert in these fields, she is a frequently invited to lead and participate in panels and consortiums. Her communication challenges, as she entered communication style coaching, were varied and ranged on the one hand from a nervousness about speaking to groups, to the unusual fear of being so good as a speaker that she would be asked to return to the podium. Indeed, her highly valued insights and unique perspective on the technology boom had produced both a positive recognition and negative anxieties surrounding her communication concerns. Her formal coaching was brief and lasted only few months. Her informal learning has gone on for several years as her professional responsibilities have increased. Her style words are *personable* and *engaging*. This is her reaction to communication style coaching:

"Communication style coaching has proven to be one of the most valuable personal and professional development efforts in my career. I have become more confident in my competence. I have found comfortable ways to express my views and accept and understand the views of others. Dennis Becker taught me to how to consider others point of view and how to make my messages, and the delivery of these messages, more relevant to

them. This is the essence of persuasion, and the basis of respect.
There is no more important business, or life, skill."

Mike is president of international business for one of the worlds largest and most influential medical device companies. He has risen through the ranks of his company over fifteen years of service in a variety of functional roles including sales, marketing, and staff development. He is a well-liked and knowledgeable member of the organization. He came to communication style coaching partially as an example to encourage his staff to voluntarily engage in the coaching. His experimental example proved so valuable to him that he subsequently assigned key individuals to go through the coaching. In addition, his learning has helped people throughout the organization as a result of his own career planning and by senior management's recognition of his people development skills and his ability to move through the internal politics found in most large organizations. His formal communication style coaching lasted one year. His informal coaching has never stopped over many years. His style words are *authoritative* and *approachable*. His reaction to communication style coaching is:

> *"I've always felt capable of communicating well with people, and I guess I did fairly well. When I began to learn what I didn't know, it was a game changer for me. I was able to both capitalize on my natural style as well as learn the techniques that complimented that style. Of particular value to me both at work and at home has been understanding the differences between the two patterns of reasoning. My ability to both recognize them and, more importantly, to adjust to them, has made a world of difference in my ability to connect with others, which is one my favorite things to do."*

Michelle is based in the United Kingdom and came to her position of marketing director in a major healthcare company. She came to her current role after a successful career in the women's fashion and beauty industry. She is also the youngest person to engage in communication style coaching. Her quick rise to an influential position prompted her need to gain control over her communication style. While she was a popular and respected member of the company, she did not have an understanding of her communication assets or needs. Yet her rise in the organization required her to interact with senior management personnel and motivate those who were reporting to her. Her communication style words are *approachable* and *authoritative*. Her formal communication style coaching lasted approximately one year. Her informal coaching has lasted several years. Her reaction to communication style coaching is:

> *"I feel very fortunate to have been able to go through this coaching at this early stage in my career. It has helped me see people in a different light and be able to identify their needs. Then, of course, be able to demonstrate the appropriate skills to help them or the project. My role requires me to interact with people from many different cultures and communication styles. With the knowledge I have gained through both the techniques I have learned, and through observing how the coaching was conducted, I have picked up so much more than I expected or, perhaps, than was intended. I am very grateful for having this continuing opportunity."*

Margie is the director of training for one of the worlds largest makers of shoes for both men and women. The company is based in London. She is based in the company's North American headquarters. She is a vibrant and charismatic personality whose energy permeates the organization. Her interest in communication style coaching was not so much for her as for those she was charged with developing. She was responsible for introducing communication style coaching to the organization's senior management level. In addition, the coaching was conducted with the second tier directors and mangers who were being developed for leadership within the company, worldwide. The formal communication style coaching lasted approximately one year. The informal coaching had been conducted with key persons over many years. Margie's reaction to communication style coaching is:

"Communication training and coaching for our people has proven to be one of the most valuable and practical training we have ever provided. After all, it does deal with what they do every day, whether with customers or fellow employees. Dennis Becker crawls into your company's skin and leaves you looking and feeling like you've gotten a communication facelift. He quickly gets the feeling of the company's culture and then takes it from there. Our district and regional managers are using his communication protocols to delegate, have difficult discussions with employees, coach and problem solve. They take the communication styles of their employees and bosses into consideration, interface that data with their personal communication style, and effect positive outcomes. It has given us meaningful and user-friendly solutions to age-old problems."

Mohamed is the director of real estate investment for the worlds largest investment company located in the Middle East. He was referred for communication style coaching by the director of human resources for his company. This HR Director had referred many other individuals to the same coaching, but Mohamed was a special case. He was responsible for billions of dollars in real estate investment around the world. An effective communication style was critical to the continued success of the organization. While his technical skills were unchallenged, his communication style was assessed to be too aggressive for his role. As part of the normal initiation of coaching, we determined that his normal aggression was actually a good thing for the work he did. However, it had diminishing returns. He was not building trusting relationships for long term developments. His style words are *authoritative* and *persuasive*. While this combination may sound like a continuance of an aggressive style, he also possessed a very engaging communication style that allowed him to establish positive relationships, but without being able to retain them. His formal communication style coaching lasted twelve weeks. His informal coaching is still going on and will probably continue for a year more. His reaction to communication style coaching is:

"I always thought that the aggressive style was positive because it got me results. What it didn't do was help me build on those results for future business. This coaching, while it feels different to me, is proving to be very effective. I see the difference in people when I interact with them now. I am more convinced that this has been a good career development move for me. I am looking forward to learning more and refining my ability to pass it on to those whom I am responsible for bringing into leadership roles."

Catherine is the director of investor relations for a leading global private manager of fixed income and credit instruments. Her firm's assets under management total approximately $20.3 billion. Catherine's role in building and maintaining relationships is crucial. She has a widely mixed group of listeners. Catherine is in her thirties. For a younger woman, working with clients that are often led by older men can be intimidating. It can be hard to maintain a sense of legitimacy in front of such a group. Projecting confidence, engaging comfortably in dialogue, and building trust are all parts of everyday communication for Catherine. Her style words are *knowledgeable* and *engaging*. Her reaction to communication style coaching is:

"Monica brought up the idea of style words when we first began working together, and I've found them helpful not only in establishing the tone of a presentation but as a sort of touchstone to help me keep the presentation on track. At the same time, an element of performance exists in every presentation we give—whether it be one on one or to a large audience. One of the keys to a successful presentation is giving a performance without losing authenticity, and style words allow the speaker to do this by picking the words she would like others to use to describe her. I picked knowledgeable and engaging, and every time I start a presentation, I think of these words. It is sort of a ritual that gets me into character but also allows me to be myself because they are words of my choosing.

"I think it is smart that Monica begins instruction with style words. For example, in order to convey to my listener that I am knowledgeable and engaging, I need to avoid tentative language and uptalk, organize my thoughts in a cohesive pattern, and use the four e's to better connect with my listener. It becomes automatic and subconscious over time, but the process works because of the style words."

Steve is a managing director of one of the worlds largest real estate investment firms. This firm prides itself in investing in unique properties. He is building relationships with every conversation he has. He has a variety of functional roles including sales, marketing, and growing the staff. His formal style coaching lasted two years. He and his team call on me each year to prepare for several important meetings. His style words are *credible* and *engaging*. His reaction to communication style coaching is:

"I believe I'm a decent public speaker, but communication coaching has helped me take that to the next level, both in terms of helpful approaches to preparation of the content, as well as techniques for improving my delivery. Moreover, beyond public speaking, Monica's thoughtful input has been helpful in the evolution of my communication style. I've been promoted and am taking on additional responsibility. Attention to some more subtle verbal and nonverbal behaviors has improved how colleagues view my confidence and authority.

"Annually, we hold a meeting for investors that often showcases members of the team who are not regular or confident public speakers. I have seen the marked improvement that has resulted from communication coaching. Feedback from the coach takes into account each individual's personality and level of confidence. The presentation content is reviewed and adjusted—but the credibility of the speaker has a notable impact on investors' perception of our firm's progress and the depth

and skill of our team. Even speakers who were initially reluctant about coaching have remarked about the positive experience, and investors have given increasingly positive feedback on the presentations each successive year."

Rick is the chief financial officer for an American based business process software provider. This company's products focus on business decision management. The company focuses on business agility and empowers leading organizations to rapidly close execution gaps and seize new opportunities. This requires senior leadership to be able to deliver a message in a clear, succinct, and motivational manner. In this type of work environment, there is very little time to make your point and first impressions matter greatly. Rick needed to choose style words that would assure he focused on key points in a logical manner. His style words are *insightful* and engaging. His reaction to communication style coaching is:

> *"Style coaching has unlocked the mysteries of how to focus and deliver a succinct and engaging presentation as well as exude credibility, confidence and congeniality. A focus on style empowered me to engage a listener with conviction. Style coaching has also helped me capture the nuanced differences in professional interactions between cultures."*

Paula is senior vice-president in a global financial institute. In the past eighteen years she has worked her way into a position of leadership, mentorship, and respect among her peers. As one of the global leaders in the finance world, she has utilized her work with style coaching for several years with much success. We first met when she was an individual contributor. Her style words were based around building her confidence and projecting gravitas. Here she speaks about a time in our coaching when her style words were *approachable* and *authoritative*:

> *"With respect to style words, the one that has resonated with me the most over the years is approachable. That might not*

sound like much, but the distinction between being friendly and being approachable, to me at any rate, is that when you're approachable, you've (internally, at least) established a level of seniority or accomplishment: you're happy to share the knowledge and wisdom that you have amassed as a means to help others grow. I think about that mostly in the everyday communication. I really encourage junior people participate on panels and so forth whenever possible—and I make myself do so as well—even if it's not a marquee event, to get that practice, so when the big moments come, you are better prepared."

Roger is an international thought leader. As a managing director for a global investment firm and owner of a major sports team in the United States, he is in the media on almost a daily basis. His communication style is regularly used as an indicator of many other aspects of his professional and personal life. Preparing for media interviews, speaking at global events, and dialoguing with heads of countries all require the ability to be clear, concise, and authentic. He is aware that his ability to build trust and rapport with listeners is what drives his success. His communication style is critical to this, of course. His style words are *authoritative* and *dynamic*. Typical of his style are his comments in reacting to his communication style coaching:

"Talking to the media on television—requires you to think about a lot of things—what you're volume is, nervous habits, what you look like or how you come across. In general, I've become a more effective communicator—more dynamic, more efficient with my comments [and in] media appearances—internally and externally with investors, media, and the world. Concentrating on my communication style keeps me consistent and focused. Overall, I am a better communicator."

Gregory is the chief research officer of an international information and data research business. He regularly communicates with people in his company, in the industry, customers, vendors, and others from around the world.

His high profile position requires both accuracy and credibility. He wants to be able to communicate his information in a compelling and respectful manner. Simply preparing a report and presenting the numbers is not effective in his world. In addition, Gregory is responsible for developing and motivating his team. His selected style words are *insightful* and *charismatic*. Here is his reaction to communication style coaching:

> *"Speech communication has a lot of variability. Each group, each person is unique in many ways. You must be able to vary your approach and you message to best suit the way in which that group will understand and or accept it. It is important that I be poised, not get ruffled, engage my listeners, and not just read the slides. This is super critical. Our data will speak for itself but to be able to tell the story in a way that engages people in various industries and the media is critical. It's cornerstone-level stuff and that's why we invest in this communication style training."*

These are a few people who are representative of the many who have and are going though communication style coaching. We have selected these as a cross section of gender and business environments. You will notice that both Mike and Michelle have chosen the same two style words, *authoritative* and *approachable*. They are quite different people. Yet the style words are the same. In both instances, they were in search of similar results. In both instances, the same words were justified. In both instances, the communication techniques learned were different. They are different people. Their work situations are different. Their personalities and learning styles are different. This is not uncommon. *Authoritative* and *approachable* are very popular communication styles for those in leadership positions. However, individual variables dictate the choice of communication techniques taught and learned. This is why it is so important that the coach and the coachee be very clear with each other in the initial phase of communication style coaching when it comes to the selection of style words.

This learning experience is customized to each person. Nothing in it can be planned in advance. It does not contain the same readings, exercises, and approaches for everyone. Every case is different. In an odd way, it is perfectly justified to say that the coach will make it up as he or she goes along. Of course, we don't mean that in its most extreme interpretation. The coach must have a very strong founding in interpersonal and intrapersonal education, communication, and coaching skills. As the relationship between the coach and coachee progresses, the needs and subsequent coaching must adjust. So it is entirely possible that two individuals will choose the same style words, but the techniques taught and learned may be different. These comments are typical of the reactions that clients have had to their individualized communication style coaching.

CHAPTER 7
SUMMARY AND RECOMMENDATIONS

A discussion about style in almost any field promotes subjective and re-actionary dialogue. Everyone has an opinion on whatever the topic seems to be. It's akin to the old adage, "Beauty is in the eye of the beholder." Communication style is certainly no exception. In many ways, because it is such a personal topic, because it can easily be linked to personality, because it can have a dominating effect in creating the opinion regarding a person, because it can determine the success or failure of projects both large and small, and because it is one of the most important connectors in human re-lationships, communication style coaching that helps individuals strength-en the impression they create with others is one of the most critical areas of personal and professional development.

Technology of all kinds is gaining an ever-stronger hold on our life-style. It is almost unthinkable not to have a cell phone. Even those the bulk of whose lives were spent in a time of one phone per household, one car per household, writing letters to friends, walking to the cor-ner mail box, and using a manual typewriter that didn't need a battery, even these folks are being compelled to embrace the cell phone and computer. It is still unknown where this tectonic shift in lifestyle will take society. It is certain that the forms of human communication are changing to incorporate and adapt to technological changes. Still, the impact and importance of pure human communication cannot be overestimated. Person-to-person communication and the development of personal relationships move the world in a unique way. People connecting to people in the most human manner, speaking and listening, will remain the essential fodder of evolution.

Ironically, as the human race moves ever close to homogenization and generic characterization, the ability to control individual communication style and personal impression becomes more significant in the effort to be yourself. Just as discoveries of DNA and genome markers draw us closer to each other, so the ability to control personal traits and communication style becomes more valuable to preserving the humanness of each person.

The future of our species and our society will be shaped by technology and personal interaction. There must be a place in our educational system where personal communication style will be a mainstream subject. Current meager efforts to teach public speaking, for example, to help students become creatively expressive, are far too minuscule for meaningful human development. The majority of these efforts happen far too sporadically and with inconsequential support. There must be a concentrated effort, which needs to begin in the earliest grades and follow through into high school years. Teaching our young people to communicate in a human manner that recognizes differences, values the humanity of others, and enables them to listen and interact with empathy and understanding is inherent in communication style teaching. This will not be in an effort to standardize or categorize individuals but rather to help each of us capitalize on, strengthen, and maintain a communication style that identifies us as unique and productive members of the world society. Without human communication there will be no meaningful and livable world society.

Communication style coaching gives every individual the opportunity, guidance, and encouragement to be the best and most effective human communicator that he or she can be.

Made in the USA
Monee, IL
10 October 2020

44420915R00056